AN ORCHESTRA
OF VOICES

AN ORCHESTRA
OF VOICES ─────────────

Making the Argument for
Greater Speech and Press Freedom
in the People's Republic of China

Sun Xupei
EDITED BY ELIZABETH C. MICHEL
With the assistance of Eric B. Easton

PRAEGER

Westport, Connecticut
London

Library of Congress Cataloging-in-Publication Data

Sun, Hsü-p'ei.
    An orchestra of voices : making the argument for greater speech and press freedom in the People's Republic of China / Sun Xupei ; edited by Elizabeth C. Michel, with the assistance of Eric B. Easton.
        p.   cm.
    Includes bibliographical references and index.
    ISBN 0–275–96956–8 (alk. paper)
    1. Freedom of the press—China. 2. Government and the press—China. I. Title: Speech and press freedom in the People's Republic of China. II. Michel, Elizabeth C., 1951– III. Title.
PN4748.C5S86 2001
323.44'5'0951—dc21   00–032375

British Library Cataloguing in Publication Data is available.

Library of Congress Catalog Card Number: 00–032375
ISBN: 0–275–96956–8

First published in 2001

Praeger Publishers, 88 Post Road West, Westport, CT 06881
An imprint of Greenwood Publishing Group, Inc.
www.praeger.com

Printed in the United States of America

The paper used in this book complies with the Permanent Paper Standard issued by the National Information Standards Organization (Z39.48–1984).

10 9 8 7 6 5 4 3 2 1

To the young journalists of China

Contents

Preface

As I review the experiences of my past, I am strangely aware—as if for the first time—that my life has been hard. My constant, visceral determination to reason toward truth is probably the reason I have survived.

Since my early childhood in a small village in Anhui Province, I had a compelling desire to go to school.[1] But my family had been poor for generations, and poverty made many things impossible. A terrible flood had washed away our simple house in 1949, so my family lived in the halls of a public building. Most of the time we ate turnips with a bit of rice. The few coins required for a semester's school supplies might as well have been a hundred. How I envied the other children as they went in to learn.

When my parents realized the persistence of my yearning, they agreed to let me go to school. We could not afford fountain pens, so for the six years of primary school I had to use either an awkward brush pen[2] or one with a nib that was fixed into a holder and then dipped in an ink pot.[3]

There was no electricity in the countryside. By fourth grade, I was expected to bring my own kerosene lamp and lampshade. The wick of the kerosene lamp came out of a small slot shaped like a horse's mouth. If I was very careful, I could economize on kerosene by picking the wick or rolling it downward and adjusting the flame to the size of a pea. My little lamp glimmered just like a firefly.

In six years of primary school, I was able to buy a snack only once. I had saved two cents for a piece of lotus root. I had seen a piece of it snapped in two and yet still remain whole, and the street merchant's magic had captivated me.

Once, a special excursion into the town of Gaohe was organized as a reward to the highest achievers. There, we were offered Chinese buns for lunch. I ate only two buns because I dreaded being asked to pay for what I knew I could not afford.

If my parents were frustrated and depressed by their financial circumstances, my academic achievements always comforted them. They deeply appreciated the great effort I made. How happy my family was when they heard that I passed the junior middle school entrance examination. By scraping together or borrowing everything we could, we collected twenty yuan[4] for my middle school tuition. As poor peasants, however, my parents had to struggle for what bread they had, and they found it impossible to support my continuing education. On the first day of the second semester of grade seven, I had to withdraw from school.

Since my household and food supply records remained at the school, I still had to go there every month to pick up my grain coupon. One of those times, less than a month before the end of the second semester, I unexpectedly ran into the head teacher, Xu Fengqi. He knew me from the first semester when I had won first place in the all-school math competition and second place in Chinese composition. When he heard that I had left school for nearly a term because of limited family finances, he suggested that I think about what my family had of value that might be equivalent to fees. In any case, he told me to come to school and resume my studies the very next day. I happily ran home to tell my parents the news.

The next day, my elder brother drove an old, emaciated sow to school as partial payment of my fees. I was able to sit in class again. Only twenty days were left in the semester, and I began immediately to hand-copy the work I had missed. A thick calcium deposit remains on the right side of my right hand's middle finger as a permanent souvenir of my hard work.

It was winter, and when head teacher Xu saw me come into the classroom without socks he bought me two pairs with his own money. For several decades, I regarded those two pairs of socks as the most precious gifts I ever received. Since the early 1980s, I have called on this respected teacher many times. I have never forgotten that my schooling would have ended long ago without his help.

In 1960, I completed junior middle school, and my score on examinations permitted me to attend Huaining High School in Huaining County. With two of my classmates who were also from poor peasant families, I walked the forty kilometers to town. We carried our luggage on shoulder poles. We had no way to buy anything to eat,[5] so we struggled through every step with empty stomachs. After twenty-nine hours of walking, we finally arrived at the Huaining High School and found something to eat.

During these high school years, my family was still short of money, so I would earn my school fees by carrying some of my mother's hot chili the forty kilometers from home to Anqing City to sell. With little or nothing of my own to eat, I would be exhausted. One time, I met a kind worker on the road. He let me put my chili on his handcart.[6] I walked weakly behind and just helped to push when the cart was going up a hill.

Near the end of one of these long walks, I decided to spend the night on the huge Yangtze River dike. I did not want to waste a single cent on accommodations. When I woke up, I realized that a thief had cut open the pocket of my trousers and taken the few coins I had earned and the ferry ticket to reach the county town. I was so depressed that I almost cried.

The China of my high school years was going through a tough period.[7] The government controlled the grain supply and encouraged people to eat wild vegetables instead. By the end of each morning's final lesson, my stomach was rumbling with hunger. A wave of excitement would sweep my heart when I heard the sound of the big food container being dropped in the corridor.

Even though it meant a hard life, I insisted on pursuing my studies. In grade ten, we began the required three years of foreign language study. Students in our school learned Russian. But, halfway through the second semester, our foreign language classes were abruptly stopped. Without certification for completing the full foreign language unit, we would not be permitted to take the university's entry examination. I discussed the matter with my classmates and wrote a complaint[8] to the Anhui Province Education Department, suggesting a remedial program that would enable us to make up our foreign language lessons. The complaint bypassed local authorities and could have caused a lot of difficulty for me. Fortunately, the education department eventually accepted our reasonable suggestion and decided that in addition to our normal class loads, we would complete the Russian language course of studies in one year.

Those years in China have been described as a time when "the strong one was exhausted to become the weak, and the weak one was consumed to become nearly dead." Despite this, I studied day and night, and I completed my high school years with top grades. After passing my qualifying exams, I was admitted to the foreign language department of Anhui University in early 1963.

My family's economic situation was no better during my university years, but the university's grant-in-aid system solved the immediate problem of feeding myself. The other obstacles were not so easily overcome.

My special field was to be English, and because of my entrance marks, I was appointed a monitor. Unlike the other students, who had studied English in high school, I had studied only Russian. From the first day, I got no better than average marks of "3." Ever since I was a little boy, I had been at the top of my class—now, as a class monitor, how could I lag behind? I made a firm resolution. In the dead of night I pricked my finger and used the blood to write in my notebook four characters that meant "Face the wall for five years!"[9] From that moment, I was diligent in my studies day and night, learning all of the grammar in the textbook and mastering the meanings and functions of the words we learned. At the end of the semester, though I weighed a few kilograms less than before, I was the only one to achieve the mark of "5" for high distinction.

Unfortunately, that year was the onset of a period of political upheaval. I had been at university for only a year when my course of study was interrupted. We students were dispatched to a rural area to participate in labor, after which came a half year of "socialist education"[10] in the countryside.

No sooner had we returned to school from the countryside than the Cultural Revolution erupted. If social programs were fundamental to the welfare and progress of our country and its citizens, then the Cultural Revolution was a disaster for China, for it abandoned China's young scholars. My five-year resolution was impossible to realize by any means.

In the earliest stages of the Cultural Revolution, I followed the general trend with full enthusiasm. It was a period of boundless worship of Chairman Mao. Acting on the Chairman's exhortation to establish ties with other revolutionaries by visiting different places,[11] I arrived in Tienanmen Square in Beijing. I used red powder mixed with water to write in my notebook, "Be loyal to Chairman Mao forever." Some of the Red Guards wrote their oaths with the red powder scraped from the walls of the Tienan Gate itself.

And yet, the more the movement went on, the more questions I started to have:

Why did the pre-Revolutionary Extraction Theory[12] persist and take so many inconsistent forms? The new version of the theory said, "If the father is a hero, his son is assumed to be a good man," and, conversely, "If the father is not a revolutionary, his son can be assumed to be a bastard." If these principles guided us, why was I denied permission to join in the

Red Guard and study Chairman Mao just because the girl with whom I shared a desk in school was my good friend? They said she was the daughter of a Black Category.[13] (Her father was an Anhui University professor and so, with the landlords, the rich farmers, the counterrevolutionaries, and the Rightists, he was treated as a reactionary during the Cultural Revolution.)

Why was the leader who had exaggerated crop yields in Anhui Province during the Great Leap Forward allowed to get off scot-free?[14] Yet Li Baohua, a good and respected leader or "blue sky"[15] who had come to Anhui to correct Leftist mistakes, was ultimately paraded through the streets night and day and publicly denounced.

Why on earth were some of the leading cadres manipulating declamatory slogans, and thus fomenting discord throughout the entire nation? Throughout our history the most enlightened emperors have known that "popular feelings may be utilized"[16] and, conversely, that "the common aspirations of the people may be feared."[17] Discord was rampant, from "denouncing with the pen" to "struggling with weapons." The country was being thrown into increasing confusion, and people were heavy hearted. Still, certain party leaders pronounced, "The situation is getting better every day!" I began to grow concerned as I watched the new politics unfold and work its effect on the country.

From the time I was small, I have been a ponderer. Like Socrates, I am always thinking and questioning, even if to no conclusion. In high school, the study of dialectical materialism fascinated me.[18] I wore out the textbook. Dialectical materialism taught me how to think and often enlightened my reasoning when I was perplexed.

As I applied my knowledge of history and politics through the lens of dialectical materialism to ponder these current matters, I became increasingly aware that this particular revolutionary movement would have even graver consequences for the country than had the Anti-Rightist Campaign or the Great Leap Forward.[19] I sensed that I should no longer be carried along with the tide, and I began instead to think for myself. I stopped participating in the factional strife of the Red Guards, ceased my vehement writing, and threw away my notebook. During the summer and fall of 1967, I found an aged teacher, concentrated on learning French, and waved farewell to the fanatical mass campaign of the Cultural revolution.

In the autumn of 1968, I returned to Anhui University, where I stayed until I graduated. I was immediately sent to a coal mine called Yuanzhuang in the Huaibei coal mining bureau in Anhui Province. There, I was first a teacher, then a coal miner, then a translator of technical information, and finally, a correspondent. Unlike working in a big city, there were few political guidelines, and I depended on my own judgment. As a guiding principle, I decided to do my best to promote the unity of people and the development of production and all but ignore the "revolutionary struggles" and political hypocrisy.[20]

When I first arrived in Yuanzhuang, I found that the two political factions [of the Red Guard] had developed an alliance in the city of Anhui. However, in nearby Xuzhou, those same two groups were still extremely antagonistic. Just as I got there, the leaders of the fighting Xuzhou factions had been dispatched to Yuanzhuang to learn harmonization.

On behalf of the children in the Red Guard and Little Red Guard, I was asked to draft a letter to facilitate the reconciliation. I was vehemently opposed to the new Cultural Revolutionary spin as it appeared in the "eight-legged essay,"[21] which was riddled with exaggerations, formulas, empty words, and Mao quotations. Instead, I worded the whole epistle as if it were written by the children themselves, reasoning that, as uncles and aunts would hope their nieces and nephews would be kind to one another, the children would expect their uncles and aunts to do the same.

When the letter was read aloud, the simple truth and genuine humanity of the "children's" voice moved the Xuzhou people. They burst into enthusiastic applause, reconciled, and even carried the letter back to Xuzhou to read to the rest of their people.

That letter changed my life. For the next five years I worked as a correspondent for the news office of the mine until, in 1975, I was moved to the Huaibei Mining Bureau news office to run the local daily paper, *Huaibei Kuanggong Bao*.

Following Einstein's assertion that truth has a simple character, I resolved to ignore the era's deliberately obfuscated theory of class struggle and stick to the practical work of covering news that would inform the production of coal. The construction of a new nation and the welfare of her people urgently needed a large quantity of high-quality coal.

In those days, the press was required to follow events closely,[22] to be prepared to follow the Party's Central Committee, and to adjust quickly to political changes.[23] My plan was to "put on the boots"[24] but still "wear the hat"[25] by politely couching important news within a current political formula. I refused to wrack my brains to compose an article based on politics that might change the following week.

Once I was directed (as were all newspapers) to denounce Deng Xiaoping, who at the moment was being criticized as "the [ill] wind" that reversed a policy of the Gang of Four.[26] The Gang of Four was manipulating the press at that time, and only articles that aligned with their views could be published. To satisfy the political formula, I wrote the headline "Striking Back the Wind of Deng's Activities of Reversing a Verdict."[27] However, the main body of the article—which should have judged a list of Deng's actions—did not mention even one.

Another time, I was coerced into participating in an anti-Deng writing group that had been established by the Huaibei Municipal Party Committee at the direction of higher authorities. There was no way to avoid participating, but once we gathered, we discovered that all four of us shared the same misgivings. Amused at the discovery, we mischievously knelt beside our hotel beds and, with hands folded at our waists, bowed and muttered, "Your Excellency Deng, we are sorry, but we have to criticize you now." Eventually, we gathered up old newspaper and magazine issues, and each of us perfunctorily copied a paragraph to improvise an article that could be turned in.

In the last years of the Cultural Revolution, I had many dangerous one-on-one discussions with friends[28] about the Haipai's[29] apparent control of the Central Committee. Under their dominion, one of China's most beautiful plays, *Yuanding Zhi Ge*, had been criticized and banned, as were most of the classic stories. I was deeply affected by this and longed for the opera of my home in Anhui, *Tianxian Pei*, to be seen by the people again. So when I heard that a banner saying "Down with Zhang Chunqiao"[30] had appeared on a Nanjing train, I began to burn with righteous fervor. Soon I would hear a poem read out during the April Fifth Campaign in Tienanmen Square[31] that criticized the Gang of Four in metaphor. The poem spoke of the people's worry for China's future and expressed their love for the motherland. I hand made private copies of the poem and passed them on to others.

During those years, I was never informed against for treasonous or offensive talk and activities. That may have been because, as a person on the front line of coal mining, I recognized full well that this "revolution" would sabotage production and wreak dire consequences. It may have been because of my Huaibeinese plain and honest nature and intuitive understanding. It may have been because I was fortunate to live among true and honest friends. For the past twenty years, those Huaibei fellows who know the value of protecting people who speak according to fact have been guests of honor in my family.

During some of those early conversations, I began the thinking that would shape the next years of my life. The simple force of one person's mistake, or even the coercion of an ambitious few, could not explain why so many preposterous political campaigns could have snowballed into an avalanche that buried a society. Our whole nation—all of us—should ask ourselves, why did we, caught up in the revolutionary rhetoric, never think it through on our own? After the successive falls of Lin Biao[32] and the Gang of Four, the question I considered most was this one: Following Lin Biao's fall from power, how could the Chinese people continue to endure identical outrages from the Gang of Four for another five years?

In 1972, I wrote a long news dispatch: "One Profound Revolution of

Thought." The story described how the Yuanzhuang coal mine recovered from the years of Lin Biao's disastrous "control, block, and press"[33] policy. Yet the minute the enterprise was stable again, the Gang of Four's renewed ideological front set off a new wave of practices that undermined effective business management. The Yuanzhuang mine relapsed into chaos until the fall of the Gang of Four, when the business was once again put back on schedule.

Where did the crux of the problem lie? Sometimes I lay awake all night, turning the questions over and over in my mind. In June 1977, at two o'clock one morning, it suddenly struck me. Although the system had been cleansed of Lin, the arguments against him had failed to neutralize a critical persuasive device, thus allowing the Gang of Four to continue using it to accomplish their own ends. Both Lin and the Gang of Four had depended on being perceived as "the Left"[34] to build their following. Therefore, the Chinese political preference for "being left rather than right,"[35] cultivated over many years, sustained them. I immediately spread out paper and scribbled an article titled "A Comparative Criticism of the Extremely Left Pretense of the Gang of Four with Its Exceedingly Right Substance."

By the time the sun rose, the paper had been written and polished. My friends read it and concurred, saying, "[This writing] represents the words that are on everyone's heart, but not yet under a single person's pen." I made copies of the essay and mailed them to the Central Party School, the Institute of Philosophy in the Chinese Academy of Social Sciences, *Red Flag* magazine, Xinhua News Agency, and *The People's Daily*. My article's main focus was the Gang's pretense at being "extremely left."

Two months later, Hua Guofeng[36] publicly reiterated the limited prevailing viewpoint[37] that it was necessary to criticize Lin Biao and the Gang of Four's "exceedingly *right* articulation of the reactionary and revisionist line." After the speech, two of the units to which I had sent my article, The Institute of Philosophy and *Red Flag*, sent me letters suggesting that I should refute Hua's focus on the Gang's "extremely right stance." I wrote the article and sent it off.

Within a short time, the theory department of *The People's Daily* wrote to say that my essay was in galley proof and would be published. The proof they sent me barely changed a word; it still said, "Lin's criticism . . . failed to grasp the main points." I could hardly conceal my excitement. Would it actually be published?

On October 14, 1977, *The People's Daily* published "The Gang of Four's Disguised Leftist Mask and Its Exceedingly Right Substance." My article was in print. "Extremely left" was watered down to read "disguised left," but it was still a big step toward the truth. The concept of *fake Left and true Right* soon became a popular saying, and widespread discussion ensued to accurately interpret the lines of Lin Biao and the Gang of Four. Ultimately, the national press realized unanimously that Lin Biao and the Gang of Four were a group of careerists and conspirators who practiced an extremely *Left* line in politics.

The following year, 1978, a National Conference on Science was convened; it featured a discussion about a standard of truth. It was also the first year after the Cultural Revolution for recruiting postgraduate students. With the end of that horrific period, when "the golden bell was destroyed and discarded, and all the while the earthen pot was making thunderous noise,"[38] science and truth were now exalted and proud. I could see the path ahead again.

Jabbering until my lips were sore, I finally convinced the higher authorities to let me register for a postgraduate examination. While I was waiting for the results, I was called to appear before my unit leader. I knew that he wanted to promote me to deputy section chief. The honor would prevent me from pursuing graduate study.[39] When we met, I told him that although I had always venerated those officials who were devoted to their public careers and diligent in serving the people, I was more interested in studying science and seeking truth. I told him that in the ten years of the Cultural Revolution, lies had become the passport of deception; whereas truth had been relegated to an inscription on its own tombstone. At present, I argued, the country's future hinged upon the success of scientific study.

When I took the national graduate entrance exam, the subject of the required political essay was "I love journalism under the Party's leadership." I wrote with emotion:

The proletariat press is a flame that burns with truth, lighting the way of liberation for the working class. From *The New Rhein*[40] on the bank of the Rhein, to *The Truth*[41] along the Seine, to the *Xiangjiang Review*[42] beside the Xiangjiang River, the proletariat's press must always express the voice and the hope of the people.

During the ten years of the Cultural Revolution, the press was used against the people. *Red Flag* magazine became a blasphemy on the red flag, and *The People's Daily* did not serve the people. Why had all this happened? With that question, my work began.

In 1978, I entered the department of media in the graduate school of the Chinese Academy of Social Sciences. My research started with the issue of press freedom. Although freedom of the press and freedom of speech and publication are safeguarded by the constitution, few if any published theses on the subjects existed and certainly no theoretical models. Knowing full well that it was risky, I chose the topic for my master's thesis. My 80,000-character thesis, "Opinions on Socialist Press Freedom," was well received by my instructors.

After I completed the master's degree, I worked as a reporter for *The People's Daily* for two and a half years. During that time, I continued my research, probing the issues surrounding freedom of the press. I also explored press reform within the framework of press freedom and related legislation. This led me to study the major inconsistencies between press theory and practice. Those articles now appear as the first seven chapters of this book.

The academic community ultimately endorsed "Opinions on Socialist Press Freedom," and its premises were included in four books. In 1984, I launched *The Journal of Press Law*, the first publication on press law. My book, *New Journalism Theories*, summarized my major research conclusions. Those theories have been positively received in both China and other parts of Asia.

Early in my graduate work, a classmate warned that my theories would cause me trouble. He was prescient. But the past thirty years have proven these issues to be of great significance to China's stability and development. Although they have frequently caused controversy, my views have been validated by the unfolding press reforms that they predicted.

In the field of social science—especially journalism, which in China relates so closely to politics and community—researchers should feel responsible to their society. I believe that the development of China's press should find its own way. The process demands that we preserve and adopt that which is best for our people.

Young people who have heard this story of my life think that I was unduly burdened to be born at such a time. However, I believe that I was also fortunate in some respects. I believe the long period of tribulation steeled and strengthened my willpower and enabled me to overcome obstacles. From this side of those hardships—and even in the midst of them—I always knew that "from a bird's-eye view, all mountains are small."[43] Each of the obstacles was eventually surmounted.

Time and again throughout my life, I have been consumed with the single, intense desire to abide by an ancient Chinese instruction: Do not be altered in straightening or humbling circumstances; do not be led astray by wealth or high position; do not be subdued by force.[44]

In my early professional career as a grassroots reporter at *The People's Daily*, those words guided me to buy my meals according to my income. Later, in the mid-1990s, it meant that I continued to ride my bicycle to work rather than sit in the government car to which I was entitled as director of the Institute of Journalism in the Chinese Academy of Social Sciences.

Throughout the years, my greatest quality has been the ability "to ponder by oneself";

    . . . not to be altered in straightening or humbling circumstances;

... not to be led astray by wealth or high position;
... not to be subdued by force.

Sun Xupei, 2000

NOTES

1. Sun's family's village was called Village of the Sun Family *(Sun Jia Laowu)*, because members of the Sun family had lived there for generations.

2. *maobi.*

3. *zhanshuibi.*

4. Less than U.S.$3.

5. The famines resulting from the Great Leap Forward reached their peak in 1960.

6. *banche.*

7. *di biaozhun, guacai dai*, the result of the Great Leap Forward.

8. *yueji shanggao.*

9. *Mianbi wunian!*

10. *shejiao.*

11. *da chuanlian.*

12. "The theory of extraction" was a guiding principle of the revolutionaries between the 1949 liberation and the Cultural Revolution.

13. *Hei Wulei.*

14. *wufeng, sanhai.* Program administrators gave out inflated crop-yield figures, even though the people were starving to death. More than forty people in Sun's small village died during this period.

15. *qingtian.*

16. *minxin keyong.*

17. *minxin kewei.*

18. According to Sun's thinking, Marxism includes "philosophy, political economics and scientific socialism." Sun is interested only in the philosophy of dialectical materialism, Marx's synthesis of the Hegelian dialectic, and the materialism of Feuerbach and earlier philosophers, which holds that historical progress emerges from the inevitable clash of irreconcilable socioeconomic conditions.

19. The Anti-Rightist Campaign, 1957–58, began as a crackdown on intellectuals who criticized the Party during the Hundred Flowers Movement in 1956–57. The Great Leap Forward followed in 1958, virtually destroying the Chinese economy by 1960.

20. *Xianzhongxin*, the act of manipulative, overt devotion done for the purpose of ingratiating oneself.

21. *Wenge bagu*, the written examination used to recruit government officials from the Tang through the Qing dynasties.

22. *jingen.*

23. *kuaizhuan.*

24. *chuanxue.*

25. *daimao.*

26. Wang Hong Wen, Zhang Chunqiao, Jiang Qing (Mao's wife), and Yao Wenyuan.

27. *Pi Deng, Fanji Youqing Fan'anfeng.*

28. One could not speak freely with more than one person at a time. One-on-one conversation was necessary in order to avoid being "denounced by one and proved by the other" in those days of political campaigns.

29. Another name for the Gang of Four.

30. One of the Gang of Four.

31. During the Qing Ming festival honoring the dead, mass demonstrations broke out on Tienanmen Square in memory of Zhou Enlai. State militia suppressed the demonstrations.

32. Former defense minister and Chairman Mao's heir apparent, Lin Biao fell from favor during the later stages of the Cultural Revolution. He was reportedly killed in an airplane crash while trying to escape to the Soviet Union in 1971.

33. *guan, ka, and ya.*

34. *Zuo.*

35. *ningzuo wuyou.*

36. Mao's designated successor, Hua held the posts of Party chairman, chairman of the Central Military Commission, and premier after Mao's death in 1976.

37. In his report to the Plenary Session of the Central Committee at the Eleventh Chinese Communist Party Congress.

38. *Huangzhong huiqi, wafou leiming.*

39. Even after Sun was in graduate school, the head of the coal mine bureau tried to get him to return to public service to "shoulder a heavier responsibility."

40. *Neue Rheinische Zeitung* was edited by Karl Marx in Cologne in 1948 until he was expelled from Germany the following year. The name reflects the resurrection of *Rheinische Zeitung*, which Marx edited in 1842.

41. Lenin was living in Paris when he founded *Pravda* in 1912 as a legal Bolshevik newspaper in St. Petersburg, although he soon moved to Cracow to exert better control over the newspaper.

42. A Marxist magazine of the New Culture Movement edited by Mao Zedong in Changsha following the May Fourth Movement of 1919.

43. *Yilan zhongshan xiao.*

44. *Pinjian buneng yi, fugui buneng yin, weivju buneng qu.*

Acknowledgments

For her efforts in having this book published, I thank Dr. Elizabeth Cheney Michel, now a corporate communication executive in Atlanta, Georgia, and visiting associate professor of communication at Kennesaw State University. In 1994, she came to China with a delegation of communications scholars. I spoke to the group as director of the Chinese Academy of Social Sciences' Institute of Journalism, and she expressed interest in my views. A few days later, she came up with the idea—which seemed quite bold to me—to introduce my controversial book *New Journalism Theories* to Western readers.

Because of the differences in cultural traditions and the political realities between China and the United States, I was initially skeptical that this work could be completed. However, Dr. Michel never wavered in her efforts. Over the five years from 1996 to 2000, she spent considerable time, energy, and resources on this work. In the hot summers of 1996 and 1997, she came to Beijing to discuss the translation with me. I have been deeply touched by her unselfish devotion to this project. Without doubt, this book could never have been published in the United States without her. I am most fortunate and honored by her dedication and her friendship.

I also thank Associate Professor Eric B. Easton of the University of

Baltimore School of Law. He came to Beijing in 1994 and 1996 with Dr. Michel and took part in supervising the book's translation. As Dr. Michel worked, he conducted the painstaking research for most of the endnotes. Throughout, he has remained committed to the book's progress and has done much to support its publication.

Several individuals offered precious support for this work with expert commentary: Bart Fisher, Steven Fraser, and Robert Muir. The team of Chen Gengtao, Sun Hong, Pei Jianfeng, and Wei Yang completed the initial Chinese-to-English translation of my writing. My colleagues at Hong Kong Baptist University and Li Xiaoming and Li Wensheng were also of help. I thank them all.

Sun Xupei

The Eisenhower professional exchange program, People to People, is fully responsible for introducing Sun Xupei and Elizabeth Michel. The opportunities the program presented in the summer of 1994, for discussion and socialization, established the relationships that became the work. The research for this Western anthology of Sun's writings was financed by Mellon Foundation faculty study grants at Mars Hill College and by awards from the Appalachian College Association. This book would not have been possible without their generous support. Our thanks also to the Madison County League of Women Voters, Charlotte Cowser Cheney, Colonel and Mrs. Albert Becker, Dr. Fred Bentley, and Jerry and Marcia Davis for their generosity and hospitality during Sun's visit to the eastern United States in the spring of 1995. There were any number of times when this project could have been put down. It is complete because Keith and Grant Michel always assumed it would be and because of the integrity and vision of the man who wrote it.

E. C. Michel

Introduction

In China, the government keeps art, ideology and the press under tight control. In art, the policy is to "let one hundred flowers bloom." In ideology, "let one hundred schools contend,"[1] is at times allowed, particularly in economics. However, in the press, control has never been loosened. What can you do as the Director of the Institute of Journalism?

Name withheld

A retired official of the Chinese Academy of Social Sciences said these words to me a few years ago, when I was still director of the academy's Institute of Journalism. His concerns proved to be prescient. By 1994, my book, *New Journalism Theories*,[2] had been offered as evidence that I was no longer suitable for the post of institute director.

Position is not important to me. Like the words of the ancient Greek philosopher, "I would rather uncover the cause of a thing than gain a Persian throne." In the years since the Cultural Revolution, I have been particularly eager to discover why working people, who are considered to be the owners of this country, could do nothing about the rampant exaggeration and blind rule that occurred between 1958 and 1961. Instead, the press was party to this "Great Leap Forward," which destroyed the country's economy and caused hundreds of millions of people to starve to death. And how is it that during the Cultural Revolution, the press could defy public opinion and put the nation in danger for ten years?[3]

Our existing journalism theory has no answer for these questions. To the contrary, it was that flawed journalism theory[4] that supported this disastrous conduct. If we are to prevent these phenomena from recurring, and if we hope to construct and develop a socialist democracy, we must perfect journalism theory and so reform the operation of the media. For these reasons I chose to research and write on the difficult topic of freedom of the press, a forbidden subject in China

Twenty years ago, I began to study freedom of the press as embodied in the freedoms of speech and publication as stipulated in the Chinese Constitution. I then focused my research on press law, which defines press freedom. Finally, my work explored press reform within the framework of press freedom and law. In the course of my studies, I have probed into other theoretical questions and journalism practices such as news writing and reporting. I have also spent considerable time over the past years researching the development of China's press. The main conclusions of my research were collected and published in China in *New Journalism Theories* in 1994.

For twenty years, the focus of my life has been exploring the fundamental issues of China's press system: the content of its media, the models by which it operates, and the ways in which it too often ineffectively serves the people of the People's Republic. The work has been difficult and not without risk. I have discovered that it is often more difficult to find a means to convey the truth than to find the truth itself.

In the last few years, my research has received a warm response from scholars, especially younger ones. Over the years, the work has also garnered considerable criticism. Not infrequently, irate individuals with more traditional ideas have cited official documents and regulations in an attempt to prove my theories detrimental to Communist Party control over the press. I have been invited to participate in many seminars, but on several occasions, I have been refused admittance without reason. Every essay in this book has such a story.

Almost everything I have written has sounded a call for press reform. In recent years, more and more people in China have come to accept my theories, and I am gratified to see that press reforms have followed my research. Since I began my studies twenty years ago, freedom of the press in China has improved markedly. I have every reason to believe that there will continue to be gradual, steady improvement, even though it may stall or even regress a bit along the way.

Now I have compiled this new book for Western readers. It includes sections from *New Journalism Theories*, as well as four new essays on freedom of the press, press legislation, press reform, and the commercial development of China's press. The chapters are presented in the order in which they were written and, as such, reflect the progression of circumstances.

Some Western readers will think the socialist press freedom discussed here is inadequate, that such freedom is not very free at all. I do not deny this. At the same time, I do not support the view that China should imitate the American free press. Tradition and history make it impossible for China to set up a totally free press system like that of the United States.

All systems have their own strengths and weaknesses. If a press system controlled by political forces could be characterized as a huge, overbearing monster, a press system driven by commercial profits is at least a small one. Where big monsters still roam openly, people may tolerate or even praise the small monsters. But when all the big monsters become extinct, people will realize how bad the small monsters are.

Instead of choosing between two monsters, the press system in China should find its own way to reform. That way should be one with Chinese characteristics, combining the advantages of both Eastern and Western press systems. Political forces should not dominate the media; neither should economic forces. Distributed control is the better choice for China. During these next years of construction, the ruling party and the government may well make use of the media to play the main melody. At the same time, other notes should be allowed as the harmony. A scientific and rational model for media communications has not yet emerged, but it is our ultimate goal. It is also the goal of this book.

NOTES

1. The reference is to the Hundred Flowers Movement of 1956–57, when intellectuals were urged to "let a hundred flowers bloom, let a hundred schools of thought contend." The "blooming" proved to be short-lived, however, as many who criticized the Communist Party during the movement were persecuted in the Anti-Rightist Campaign that preceded the Great Leap Forward of 1958.

2. Modern China Publishing House, 1994.

3. 1966–76.

4. Theory means "premises" or "implied policies" that describe how a particular entity operates within the society. Theories come from several sources: (a) general statements by heads of state, (b) published research, or (c) government and/or Party reports on exemplary practices in specific work units.

CHAPTER 1 —————————————————

On Socialist Press Freedom

The concept of press freedom is so sensitive in China that few people are willing to talk about it. My determination to examine socialism and press freedom was born of my experience during the Cultural Revolution (1966–76), when the role played by the press resulted in calamity—both for China and for her people.[1]

In the wake of the Cultural Revolution, increasing numbers of Chinese journalists began to analyze the lessons of that social disaster. Hu Jiwei, then editor-in-chief of *The People's Daily*, pointed out soon afterward, "If we are to avoid [the Chinese idiom] 'When the Party errs along the road, the media make the same mistakes,' we Chinese journalists must hold fast to a new principle—while keeping Party leadership of the people our prime consideration, we should honor the people's needs as well." Because this statement was interpreted at the time to place public needs before Party leadership, Hu was removed from his position at *The People's Daily*.[2]

The freedoms of speech and press as articulated in the Chinese Constitution provided the logical starting point for my research.[3] The purpose of my work has been twofold: to articulate the working journalist's right to keep silent when Party leadership is ill-advised, and to show, through sound theoretical and historical reflection, that we Chinese journalists have the right to report the truth. It is this concept—reporting facts that reveal flawed policy—that some Party leaders find difficult to accept.

In all the decades since the founding of the People's Republic, the Chinese press has yet to publish even a single article dealing with socialist press freedom or how to facilitate its realization. A handful of articles have mentioned the subject, but only in the narrow context of criticizing "so-called capitalist press freedom."

This work represents a series of writings first begun in 1981; the most recent was written in 1999. When the initial articles were first completed, a friend of mine predicted they would cause me trouble. He was prescient. The writing was censored three times: (1) during the Ant-Spiritual Pollution campaign of 1984, (2) in the midst of the Anti-Bourgeois Liberalization campaign that began from the end of 1986, and (3) as part of the Mass Screening that followed the political upheaval of 1989 that culminated on Tienanmen Square.

Nevertheless, Chinese society has been making progress. Thanks to Deng Xiaoping's policies of economic reform and our opening to the outside world, this article and my other research results have been able to find their way into print, despite the fact that their publication has brought me one trouble after another. It is my sincere hope that this work will help to explain the import of the past and present upon the critical future of a Chinese, socialist, democratic, and free press.

This first article, written first in 1981, became the foundational premise of my 1993 book, *New Journalism Theories*. It maintains that China's press policies do not reflect the freedoms of press and speech guaranteed in the Constitution; discusses problems with the current press system, particularly as manifested during the Cultural Revolution; and offers general recommendations for improvement. It represents the first published articulation of these concepts.

China's Constitution provides its citizens with the freedom of speech and the freedom of publishing.[4] It naturally follows that freedom of the press is one of the civil rights of the Chinese people. By freedom of the press, I mean freedom of speech and freedom of publishing through such journalistic tools as newspapers, periodicals, radio broadcasting, television broadcasting, and news agencies.

For too long in China, freedom of the press has been regarded as a capitalist concept. As a result, many have been afraid to talk about it. Today [1981], as the Chinese people continue to tread on once-forbidden ground, freedom of the press has become a topic of increasingly heated public debate. This mind-set has triggered positive changes in the field of journalism. The changes are also the result of the serious soul-searching that followed the domestic media's negative role in China over the course of many years, a role that often brought about disastrous consequences during the Cultural Revolution.

THE CHASM BETWEEN PRACTICE AND THEORY

Let us explore two historical incidents among the many disasters brought about by the domestic media: coverage of the Tienanmen Square incident of 1976 and that of the Southern Anhui incident of the early 1940s.

April 5 is the spring date on which the Chinese annually mourn their dead. On that date in 1976, in open defiance of the Gang of Four,[5] hundreds of people in the Chinese capital converged, of their own free will, on Tienanmen to commemorate the late Premier Zhou Enlai. It was a moving demonstration of the people's concern about the future of their nation. Two days later, however, a skewed, unrecognizable story appeared on the front pages of all newspapers throughout the country. The spontaneous, open, mass activity was branded "a premeditated, planned, and organized counterrevolutionary, political incident."

This reveals two serious defects in the Chinese media of the time. First, they were able to print outright lies. Second, a fraudulent story could appear on the front pages of all newspapers, and no alternative stories would be allowed into print. In this particular incident, the blatant, stifling media censorship was of a more fascist nature than ever before in history.

During the Southern Anhui incident of the early 1940s, Kuomintang troops launched a sneak attack on Communist soldiers who were there to fight the Japanese.[6] The incident shook the world. At the time, the Kuomintang-controlled newspapers carried distorted stories, but a few newspapers, defying the threat of government closure, managed in varying degrees to print the true story.

If, as Lenin said, a socialist democracy is a million times more democratic than any capitalist democracy, how could these shocking incidents have happened? Some place the blame on a few bad eggs in the central leadership. While they certainly have a point, if that were the only reason, printed lies would strictly coincide with the times when there were bad eggs in the central leadership. Such is not the evidence of the media coverage of the Great Leap Forward.[7]

In 1958, a wave of hyperbolic coverage of everything swept all newspapers, big and small. To promote the Great Leap Forward, newspapers vied with one another to see who could invent the most astronomical agricultural-production figures. The highest actual rice output per mu of land (about one-sixth of an acre) at the time was some 500 kilograms. But from July to September 1958, news reports about "high-yielding" experimental plots incrementally put per-mu output first at 1,000 kilograms, then 4,500 kilograms, then 21,500 kilograms, and finally a shocking 65,000 kilograms. Such wild exaggerations filled the pages of national and local newspapers at the time.

Chinese peasants were infuriated by these lies, and those newspaper writers who still had consciences felt outrage. But not a single newspaper dared to puncture the lies or even express misgivings lest they be branded "doubters, onlookers, or account settlers."[8] Their misgivings were well founded. A Fujian Province reporter—who had graduated from agricultural school—saw through the madness and refused to write stories about "high-yielding fields." He was soon labeled "right-leaning ideologically"[9] and fired.

It is obvious that a situation like this happened not because bad eggs at the top wielded power, but rather because a Leftist policy line ruled the country. Repeated journalistic malpractice over these past decades shows that the Chinese media do not have the power to resist government- and/or Party-sanctioned, injurious policies.

Admittedly, it is sometimes Chinese journalists who fail to thoroughly investigate, resulting in inaccurate news stories. To be fair, though, journalists rarely deserve primary responsibility for widespread false reports. The existing structure of China's journalistic system does not provide the right to combat misguided policies, nor does it protect their freedom to report facts truthfully. Consequently, the Chinese media can do serious harm whenever certain conditions arise.

SERIOUS DRAWBACKS IN THE JOURNALISTIC SYSTEM

Were the highest authorities to adopt appropriate guiding principles and implement policies in accord with social conditions and the best hopes of the people, China's journalistic system would be superior in many respects to its capitalist system counterparts. Under such conditions, the Chinese media would play a positive role in publicizing state policies, promoting performance in all social sectors, educating the people, safeguarding public security, and cultivating social ethics.

The media did play such a role, and did it very well, during the eight years immediately following the founding of new China and particularly after 1978, when China embarked on the road to modernization through economic reforms.[10]

But the Chinese system suffers from a serious defect: It does not have the capacity to adjust itself. In cybernetic terms, it lacks a feedback-responsive adjustment function. By feedback-responsive adjustment I mean that within an automatic regulating system, not only do operational parts carry out designated performance functions, but internal conditions are fed back to the central controls which, on the basis of the feedback, make effective adjustments for individual operational parts. For example, a radio with a feedback-responsive adjustment function increases its amplification of a strong signal and decreases the volume or simply shuts off extraneous noise.

Unfortunately, China's journalistic system, like a poor radio, increases its volume when receiving good signals but continues to blast away when receiving bad signals. It is unable to decrease the volume or simply not transmit the bad signals. All the media can claim is, "If you support something, I'll do better than you in voicing support; if you are against something, I'll surpass you in opposing it." Because they cannot benefit from the feedback of public opinion, the Chinese media become impotent when confronted with unjust policies or "the wills of officials." The media can only pour fuel on an existing fire.

The relationship between misguided policies and impotent journalism is symbiotic. As a parasite requires the protection of its host to grow and reproduce, so too do flawed policies increase in influence and cause widespread damage when protected by an impotent journalistic system.

Over the years, many journalists in China have resigned themselves to the fact that their fundamental task is to unify the people's thinking with that of the highest authorities. Whether or not the media's effect is blessing or misery, then, depends upon the value of the leadership's strategies. Reporters who defend this policy say—even when they acknowledge that a published article has had disastrous effects—that the report itself was "fully justified" simply because it followed policy. Any detrimental effect is blamed on extraneous factors.

In those instances when the press has admitted the need for internal review, their findings have stopped at a "failure to tell the truth," as if the false reports provoked disaster because reporters had originally been oblivious to the fact that news must be truthful! But even when destructive policies began to come forth like a flood, reporters could not file truthful stories.

The real problem, in fact, is that when a detrimental political line held sway, journalists had no means to tell the public what was really happening, no matter how committed they were to the principle of truthfulness in news coverage. This vital issue has never been studied and resolved because—when the Party and the government began to implement beneficial policy and the media once again won the trust of people with accurate news coverage and rational commentaries—the problem was put on the back burner and then forgotten.

China has entered a new historical period. Since 1978, the Party's reform policies have once again won the trust of the Chinese people, and newspapers and radio/TV broadcasts have been able to reflect public sentiment. Isn't now the best time for us to do some soul-searching and learn from our past mistakes?

THE MEDIA FACTOR IN THE DISASTROUS CULTURAL REVOLUTION

Everyone knows that the media were instrumental in proliferating the disastrous excesses of the Cultural Revolution. Lies and inflammatory

editorials filled the newspapers; common sense and normal human behavior were cast aside; white was branded black and black, white.[11] The
Gang of Four possessed no special powers, yet by relentlessly imposing
the policy of opinion uniformity, it was able to muzzle the entire nation.
No trace of public grievances appeared in any news medium during their
tenure.

Some people argue that the media's devilish excesses during the Cultural Revolution still do not indicate deficiencies in the journalistic system. To be sure, the Cultural Revolution was largely the work of the
personality cult surrounding Mao Zedong and the disruption of Party
democratic centralism. The excesses of the Cultural Revolution were also
the result of Mao's mistakes. But Deng Xiaoping identified the root cause
when he said, "It won't solve the problem [of explaining how the Cultural Revolution happened] to talk only about Comrade Mao Zedong's
personal mistakes. What matters most is the problems of the system.
Comrade Mao Zedong advanced many good ideas, but some of our own
problematic systems pushed him to the antithesis of what he once advocated."[12] Among those problematic systems are our leadership system
and, naturally, our journalistic system.

Because our journalistic system lacks a clear-cut, scientific structure,
evil people can manipulate it. As a result, people cannot enjoy the freedoms of speech and press, rights guaranteed by the Chinese Constitution. The Cultural Revolution scenario reveals precisely the defects of
our journalistic system.

Today, the Party and government are studying political reform to ensure that the excesses of the Cultural Revolution will not recur. In the
same spirit, we too should revisit the problems in our journalistic system.
Current political system reform will not spill over into automatic solutions to the problems of the Chinese press. Though they are connected,
they are not the same. The press has distinct characteristics and follows
its own laws. Research efforts, therefore, must be concerned with not
only the working dynamic of our journalistic system and the degree to
which it effectively serves the proletariat, but also how the formal system
itself can be rational and scientific.

The purpose of such reform is by no means limited to preventing the
press from once again becoming a tool for powerful advocates of destructive political policies. With bitter lessons learned and reforms unfolding in all fields, there is an ever decreasing possibility that anything
like the Cultural Revolution will happen again. But ours is still "a country afflicted with the ills of bureaucratism." In China, we continue to see
bureaucratism and autocracy in varying forms as well as other kinds of
social evil. The perpetrators of those evils will use loopholes in our journalistic system to achieve their ends.

By the same token, reform should not be regarded solely as a means to forestall the emergence of harmful political lines and overcome bureaucratism. Freedom of the press, like socialist democracy, is an objective as well as a means to an end. Freedom of the press must be one of the people's primary objectives in their quest for a better society and a better life. Freedom of the press is the unshirkable responsibility of a proletarian Party and a socialist government. To guarantee freedom of the press for the people whom the Party and government serve is in the nature of socialism.

THE PROPER FUNCTION OF A SOCIALIST PRESS SYSTEM

The primary function of all the branches of Chinese media is to cover events and provide information. It is also important that the media ably inform the proletariat as to Party and government political lines and policies and inspire the Chinese people in their drive toward modernization. Our media should also have a third function: exposing ill-conceived political policies and official dictates that prove counter to the public welfare. This can be achieved by truthful reporting and by publishing the full spectrum of public opinion.

To effectively fulfill these three functions for the good of the state and the people, a socialist media must have relative autonomy. Socialist freedom of the press means that the media should be subject to supervision by the people, by the Party, and by law. This can best be accomplished by conscientiously serving the people within an atmosphere of responsible independence and inviolate freedom prescribed by law.

In accordance with this principle, all initial news stories and reports that cover the shortcomings or potential threats of specific policies must be freely published as long as they are truthful, do not violate law or social ethics, and do not jeopardize public interest. Neither journalists' right to work nor their political rights must be infringed upon.

In addition, a multi-tiered ownership/publication structure should be established to include Party-run newspapers, newspapers run by various institutions, and newspapers run by individual citizens.

Finally, a press law should be enacted so that journalistic practice comes under the rule of law. Such law should include (a) (as its primary function) just, certain, and measurable consequences for unethical journalistic practice, thereby serving as a deterrent to such practice; (b) the placing of sole responsibility on the authors of law-breaking articles; (c) mandatory prosecution for criminal activity; (d) the expectation of journalistic self-discipline; (e) a conscientious responsibility to the Party's and the people's integrity; and (f) public commendation for those journalistic organizations that make outstanding contributions.

This is socialist press freedom. This structure ensures that the media, subject to open supervision by the Party and the people, are not entirely an independent force. At the same time, it also provides the press with what Engels called "independence in form," which allows the press to editorially veto the publication of seriously flawed policies and/or ideas imposed from above and, subsequently, prevents the press from becoming a tractable tool of one power group or another.

WHY SOCIALIST PRESS FREEDOM? DEFINING THE PREMISES OF DISCUSSION

Freedom of the press has always been a sensitive and complicated issue. Some people in China do not approve of the term "socialist press freedom." They categorically denounce it as capitalistic and deceptive. From their point of view, whoever mentions freedom of the press is effectively espousing capitalism.

To them, "freedom" connotes irresponsible abandon—being able to do whatever one desires. Intentionally or unintentionally, they interpret freedom to mean the discarding of socialist principles, a disrespect for laws, founding newspapers without going through proper procedures, and publishing whatever materials one wants to publish. They are indignant, convinced of the veracity of their point of view, and will not have anything to do with freedom of the press. These people do not interpret the term "freedom" scientifically.

In actuality, freedom of the press is a historical movement governed by its inherent laws and by the larger law of social development. As such, it exists independently and endures, regardless of human will. Ultimately, socialism should have a more extensive and more civilized freedom of the press than capitalism.

NOTES

1. See Judy Polumbaum, "The Tribulations of China's Journalists After a Decade of Reform," in *Voices of China, The Interplay of Politics and Journalism*, Chin-Chuan Lee, ed., The Guilford Press, 1990.

2. Hu "asserted that a docile press had worked against the public interest by slavishly following the Party during the Great Leap Forward and the Cultural Revolution, and suggested that a truly socialist press owed its first loyalty to the people." Ibid.

3. Article 35 of the Constitution of 1982 provides: "Citizens of the People's Republic of China enjoy freedom of speech, of the press, of assembly, of association, of procession, and of political rights according to law."

4. Western thought assumes "freedom of publishing" as part and parcel of the freedom of speech. Here, Chinese thought and the problem at hand make it necessary to separate the two. In China, there are two points at which press freedom may come into question: the point at which the thought is expressed by

an individual or group is covered under "freedom of speech"; the point at which that expressed thought is formally published deals with the "freedom to publish." Throughout his writing, Sun's careful arguments are made according to that premise.

5. Mao Zedong's wife, Jiang Qing; Zhang Chunqiao; Wang Hongwen; and Yao Wenyuan.

6. According to official Party history, on January 4, 1941, approximately 9,000 soldiers of the Communist New Fourth Army began marching north from southern Anhui Province. On the second day, while passing through a narrow mountain pass near the town of Maolin, the unit was ambushed by 80,000 Kuomintang troops. The unit's commander was taken prisoner and its deputy commander killed. Only about 1,000 soldiers managed to break through after ten days' fighting.

7. The Great Leap Forward was Mao Zedong's attempt to jump-start industrialization in China through sheer political will. Between 1958 and 1960, an estimated 20 to 30 million Chinese died of malnutrition and famine as a direct result of Great Leap Forward policies. John King Fairbank, *China: A New History*, p. 368, Harvard University Press, 1992.

8. A "doubter" is a skeptic; an "onlooker" is much like a spy; an "account settler" would be one who used his media platform to wreck vengeance on someone in a ministry.

9. That is, from October 1949 to late 1957, when the relatively free Hundred Flowers movement gave way to the Anti-Rightist Campaign that preceded the Great Leap Forward.

10. Assistant editor's note—The Third Plenary Session of the Eleventh Central Committee in December 1978 is typically given as the beginning of China's economic reforms.

11. A collection of materials from the Chinese press in the early years of the Cultural Revolution appears in *The Great Cultural Revolution in China*, compiled and edited by the Asia Research Center, Charles E. Tuttle Co., 1968.

12. These sentiments are representative of the Party line from late 1980 through the Sixth Plenum of the Eleventh Central Committee. See Colin Mackerras et al., *China Since 1978*, pp. 22–26, St. Martin's Press, 1994.

CHAPTER 2

The Proletariat's Struggle for Press Freedom

The reason the ascendant bourgeoisie class was able to attract the laboring class to participate in its revolution against feudalism and then succeed was precisely because the bourgeoisie included in its platform universal suffrage, freedom of speech and the press, and freedom of assembly. In so doing, the proletariat made a considerable contribution to the establishment of press freedom.

Once the concept of capitalist press freedom became a factor, the proletariat began waging a new struggle for press freedom, this time against the capitalist model. The purpose of the new struggle was to prevent press freedom from becoming a ruling class privilege; to empower press freedom to facilitate the proletariat's mission.

The proletariat has always been a major force in the struggle for and safeguarding of press freedom. Marx, Engels, and Lenin all fought for press freedom. Marx began his revolutionary life by fighting for press freedom in "Comments on the Latest Prussian Censorship Instruction," "The Ban on *The Leipziger Allgemeine Zeitung*," and "Justification of the Correspondent from the *Mosel*." In these distinctive essays, freedom of the press is presented as the most basic of freedoms. Without it, Marx argued, all other freedoms are merely bubbles that burst one another as they collide; if one freedom is in question, all freedom is in question. He denounced censorship of books and newspapers by Prussia's feudal rulers, arguing they were limiting the spirit to a single form of existence. The fundamental way to cure the system of censorship, Marx maintained, was to abolish it.

Marx, Engels, and Lenin also made full use of freedom of the press as a legal weapon. They began a host of revolutionary newspapers that exposed efforts to deprive the people of freedom to publish. Engels pointed out that "Without freedom of the press, right of association and right of assembly, no workers' movement is possible. Political freedom, the right to assembly and association, and freedom of the press are our weapons."[1]

In the same way, the 1869 constitution of the German Social Democratic Labor Party pledged to abolish all legal restrictions on rights concerning the press, association, and assembly. Lenin himself advocated infinite freedom of belief, speech, the press, assembly, and association.

In China, Mao Zedong consistently made a high priority of the struggle to win the freedoms of speech, publication, and the press. In his February 1942 article "Ten Proposals for the Kuomintang," Mao demanded that the Kuomintang government "lift the ban on other parties and provide support for a free expression of public opinion." In an April 1945 speech called "On Coalition Government," Mao displayed his full agreement with Marxist thinking: "The freedoms of speech, the press, assembly, association, political conviction and religion are the people's most important freedoms." He called for the abolition of any reactionary laws and decrees that suppressed those freedoms.

A newly empowered proletariat customarily writes freedom of speech and the press into its constitution immediately upon winning power. The Soviet Union's 1934 constitution gave the Soviet people press freedom. China's 1954 constitution says, "Citizens of the People's Republic of China shall have freedom of speech, press, assembly, association, parade and demonstration." It also declares, "The state should provide those material amenities necessary to ensure that citizens enjoy these freedoms." Each subsequent Chinese constitution has included provisions for freedom of speech and freedom of the press.

This conflict is in keeping with a longstanding pattern in China. The right to speech and press freedom that is clearly written into the Constitution is seldom discussed in publications or within academic circles. Even journalism researchers have shunned the subject. When, on rare occasions, the issue has been raised, detailed discussion did not follow. Whoever writes something to discuss freedom of the press is certain to be regarded as "departing from the classics and rebelling against the orthodox" or "worrying about troubles of one's own imagining." This logic is so entrenched that anomaly is regarded as norm. Of course, this muddled situation should not seem surprising, given the nature of journalistic reform since the founding of new China.

THE HISTORY OF CHINA'S JOURNALISTIC REFORM
SINCE 1948

Our media contributed actively to socialist revolution and economic development at new China's founding and for a considerable time thereafter. The new government adopted a reasonably tolerant media policy, establishing a newspaper structure in which Communist Party newspapers and non-Communist Party newspapers coexisted, albeit with the former having a dominant position.[2] In a 1950 decision, the Central Committee of the Chinese Communist Party (CCP) declared, "Since deficiencies and mistakes in our work may easily harm the interests of the masses, it has been decided to encourage criticism of all shortcomings in our work on all public occasions, among the people, and especially in newspapers and other publications." This policy established the principle of press criticism in socialist China, a principle viewed as important to the consolidation of political power in the country.

Regrettably, however, at a time when socialist transformation of the means of production has been completed throughout the country,[3] when large-scale class struggle is a thing of the past, and when the focal point of the Communist Party's work has shifted to economic construction and the development of socialist democracy, the authorities have neglected the reform of the journalistic system and the development of a socialist press freedom. To the contrary, those who have drawn attention to this issue have been subjected to ruthless persecution. Journalistic study, including discussion of press freedom, has been suppressed.

This is part of an unfortunate pattern. As early as 1956, powerful voices for positive reform of the country's journalistic system were loud and clear. An editorial in the July 1, 1956, *People's Daily* pointed out: "*The People's Daily* is the people's newspaper as well as the Party's newspaper. . . . The people are the masters of newspapers. . . . Newspapers are the medium of public opinion." The editorial called for "broadening the scope of news coverage . . . and providing a forum for free discussion." Liu Shaoqi (later state president) put forward two proposals, one for shifting the operation of the New China News Agency to an organization other than the Party and government, and a second proposing competition among newspapers and publications.

However, as China's journalists were gathering the next year for their first Beijing forum (May 1957), the Anti-Rightist Campaign obliterated these very proposals,[4] and proponents of greater press and speech freedom were suddenly accused of "following a reactionary, capitalist, journalistic policy line." Many journalists, such as Professor Wang Zhong, who were devoted to reform or who tried to establish a socialist journalistic system, fell victim to the Anti-Rightist Campaign.

Worse was to come. After the Anti-Rightist Campaign in 1957, Leftism began to dominate journalism-related discussions. The guiding principles of "the media are a tool of class struggle" and "the media are a political tool" took on more Leftist meanings, effectively strangling journalistic study. Instead of developing in accord with objective laws for the profession, China's media found themselves in a weaker position than before 1957. Gone from newspapers were truthful reporting of news and the animated 1956 atmosphere of "a hundred schools of thought contending."

By 1958, newspapers were overflowing with grandiloquent lies, bogus news stories, and bogus photographs, thereby exacerbating the effects of the disastrous Great Leap Forward campaign. Such newspaper practices evoked bitter popular sentiment, but nobody dared to speak out. The newspapers that were intended to serve the people had become a tool that harmed them.

The disastrous consequences of these Leftist policies allowed political life in early 1962 to take a turn for the better. Journalism scholars began to study issues. Reforms in newspaper content, reporting methods, and layout were carried out, news and commentaries were more or less truthful, and newspaper supplements became more animated.

But because the Leftist standards had not been politically and ideologically discredited, journalistic studies remained superficial, and press reform was limited to trivial matters. Afraid, people consistently avoided crucial press freedom issues or anything concerning reform of the country's journalistic system.

Later in 1962, Mao Zedong called for "never forgetting the class struggle," and the people became terrified again. Soon, they would hear continuous barrages of accusations—"newspapers have been full of feudal, capitalist and revisionist black stuff' and "newspapers have been playing host to clusters of poisonous weeds." Researchers and reformers once again lost whatever enthusiasm they might have had for thought and reform.

Then came the ten years of the Cultural Revolution (1966–76), a decade when journalistic tools wrought great havoc. This too was a tragic and barren decade for the Chinese media. Newspapers were full of lies and logic-defying comments in the style of Nazi propagandist Joseph Goebbels.

All articles had the same content and style; all newspapers had the same look. Before writing a story, a reporter had to check wording and "appropriate approaches" against the standard of "the two newspapers and one journal" that carried the official line—*The People's Daily*, the

Liberation Army Daily, and *Red Flag*. Before designing layout, editors were required to call *The People's Daily*, the organ of the Central Committee of the Chinese Communist Party, for guidance in matters ranging from general layout, to the wording and placement of headlines, to the number of columns and even the sizes of print. Everything in all papers had to be exactly the same.

This was unprecedented not only in China, but also in the history of world newspaper publishing. Not a shred of socialist press freedom was to be found. In its place was a feudal, fascist, cultural autocracy and a system of press censorship more arbitrary than was Hitler's.

However peremptory a system of censorship may be, it cannot muzzle all the people. Under the rule of the Gang of Four, some Chinese journalists risked their careers to seize the occasional opportunity to slip into newspapers the truth that people expected. After the downfall of Lin Biao[5] (but before that of the Gang of Four)[6] *The People's Daily* and some local newspapers—with encouragement from the late Premier Zhou Enlai—carried articles criticizing anarchism and ultra-Leftist thinking. Although this did not last long, it was a welcome change to the depressed and idealistic.

The most important conclusion Chinese journalists can draw from their tortuous and difficult path is that there is a vast difference between writing freedom of speech and press into the Constitution and the ability to practice those freedoms. People must continue fighting for enforcement of law, possibly for a long time. And we must fight against two things simultaneously: (1) China's feudal, autocratic cultural influences and forces of habit; and (2) any tendency toward anarchy and extreme liberalism.

New China was never baptized by a bourgeois revolution, and so feudalistic ideas have continued to enjoy strong influence. For that reason, greater attention should have been paid to combating feudal, autocratic influences and the forces of habit. For a long time we failed to do so and with disastrous results. Specific lessons of recent decades prove that reforming China's journalistic system will require deliberate, defined effort.

THE LESSONS OF RECENT DECADES POINT TO REFORM

An Ziwen was persecuted by the Gang of Four. Just before his death, the former head of the Organizational Department of the Central Committee of the CCP said, "It is crucial that we earnestly study why, for ten long years, the viewpoints of the whole Party and of all the people could not express themselves openly and through normal channels."

Marx commented similarly on Napoleon Bonaparte's 1851–52 coup d'état. "It is not enough to say, as the French do, that their nation was taken unawares. . . . It remains to be explained how a nation of thirty-six million can be surprised and delivered, unresisting, into captivity by three swindlers."[7]

We too should ask. Why was China driven into utter chaos by this tiny Gang of Four? Why did a population of 1 billion feel completely powerless before their perversities? Is it because the Chinese people were gullible? Not at all.

Many people were seething with anger at the Gang's mendacity. The problem was that, under the Gang's manipulation of ingrained feudal, autocratic rule, the Chinese people lost the normal methods and tools of protest, including the right to use published public opinion to expose wrongdoing.

Looking back, we can now agree on a variety of explanations for the Gang's empowerment, any of which would support reform of both China's political system and its system of choosing Party and state leaders. Although political, ideological, and organizational explanations are valid, no one will argue with a communication-oriented explanation—that the highly centralized journalistic system completely suffocated socialist press freedom, thereby giving this gang of swindlers an effective means by which to trample the people's dreams and violate their will.

This painful history demands that our reaction not be limited to whining for justice for a handful of buffoons. Instead, this episode should compel us to actively reform our information system. Only through reform of the country's entire journalistic system can we eliminate the key contributing factor to such calamity.

NOTES

1. *Selected works of Marx and Engels*, vol. 2, p. 441, The People's Press, 1972.

2. Favorable propaganda articles on model workers made many of them household names, including workers Hao Jianxiu, Wang Chonglun, Meng Tai, Ma Hengchang, and peasant Li Shunda. But the papers also exposed corrupt officials, as in the coverage of Liu Qingshan and Zhang Zishan, leaders of the Tianjin Prefectural CCP Committee who were sentenced to death for embezzlement. During that period, the level of press freedom was appropriate to the economic conditions and the need for political power consolidation. Accordingly, newspapers played a positive role in a series of major events, including the takeover of cities by the Communist Party-led troops, the campaign to suppress counterrevolutionaries, the land reform, the movement to aid Korea in her fight against U.S. aggression, and the socialist transformation of capitalist industrial and commercial enterprises. Of course, this period also witnessed several erroneous newspaper accusations, such as those of the film "The Story of Educator Wu Xun" and of Hu Feng, a well-known writer and literary critic. These misrepresentations, however, were not typical of the mainstream press at the time.

3. "Socialist transformation of the means of production" refers to the completion of government and Party systemization of state-sponsored publication centers where news is actually printed.

4. Rightists generally favored modernization and reform. Anti-rightists opposed such change. Leftists adamantly supported the status quo of centralized power and tight control.

5. Lin was the defense minister who enjoyed the imprimatur of Mao Zedong's "comrade-in-arms and successor" during the Cultural Revolution until he split with Mao in 1971. Allegedly, Lin was killed in a plane crash while attempting to flee to the Soviet Union after a failed attempt to seize power from Mao.

6. The "smashing of the Gang of Four" occurred on October 6, 1976, when then Acting Premier Hua Guofeng arrested the four leaders of the Cultural Revolution.

7. *Selected works of Marx and Engels*, vol. 2, p. 608, The People's Press, 1972.

_____

CHAPTER 3

What Should Socialist Press Freedom Look Like?

This article was originally written in the early 1980s. Chapters 1, 2 and 3 were originally written and published at the same time. This chapter identifies four aspects of press freedom and builds reform recommendations upon what were then considered credible historical and philosophical premises.

What does socialist press freedom look like? Of what factors is it composed? A responsible description requires a thorough, theoretical examination of four issues peculiar to the Chinese question. They are (*a*) the freedom to report, (*b*) the freedom to express views, (*c*) the freedom to publish newspapers, and (*d*) the freedom to criticize.

THE FREEDOM TO REPORT NEWS

People need to know about the events taking place in their community and the world. It has always been so. The more people understand about the world and try to change it, the greater this need will be.

In the small-scale, peasant economy and political autocracy of China's feudal eras, economic and political activities were restricted and news was scarce. There was no demand for it. Since then, the emergence of a middle class, socialized mass production, the global market, and political realities have broadened economic and political activity to an unprecedented degree. As a result, economic and political news has dramatically increased. The people have had greater need for it.

From this societal evolution, the concept of "the right to know" was born. Its main precept is that the people have the right to know how the government does its job. However, simply acknowledging the people's "right to know" is futile in a culture where some leaders—who publicly affirm the people's right to know—also believe that the government and people are one and the same, as if the government were the ultimate embodiment of public opinion and even the people themselves. From that line of thinking, the government—considering itself to *be* the people—assumes "I know what is best; therefore the people never need to know, because the Party knows." This mind-set obstructs public decision making and seriously inhibits any inclination the government might have to open information channels to the public.

In a socialist society, news should be much richer, since socialism means greater economic productivity and the opening of politics to all the people, who in turn require more news to inform their economic, political, and cultural initiatives. According to Lenin, "A state is strong when the people know everything, can form an opinion of everything and do everything consciously."

Based upon the amount of knowledge potentially available to readers, people in a socialist society should have the advantage over their capitalist counterparts, for knowledge will enable them to exercise their rights as masters of society. However, the reality of a centralized press—even within socialism—is that people have precious little knowledge of issues and information. Filtered by a plethora of restrictions and unnecessary concerns, little usable news reaches the majority of China's citizens.

In the days of China's feudal society, a prevailing axiom held that "People should be ruled but not be allowed to know about things." The ruling classes knew that the best way to make people submit was to keep them ignorant. But socialism espouses democracy, and people are their own masters.

If they are not allowed to know, how can the people become masters of their country? Nor is it enough for them to know in general terms; they should know as much as possible. It is not enough for them to know only one side of the issues; they should know both the positive and negative aspects. Clear judgment comes from full understanding. Forbidding newspapers to provide news and information is the same as depriving people of their right to make considered judgments and so to participate in running state affairs.

If we are to turn these laudable democratic principles of socialism into reality, it is necessary—as the Common Program of the Chinese People's Political Consultative Conference provides—to "protect the freedom to report truthful news, [as long as that news is not] used to slander, undermine the public interest, or inflame conflict." Any truthful news should be allowed into print as long as the reporting does not violate law and public ethics. Only when this quality of freedom is realized can newspapers provide more and better information. Only then will the readership become informed.

Broadening the scope of news reporting and increasing the amount of information must be justified by one measure: To what degree does this coverage allow people to better exercise their rights as masters of their country? Correspondingly, the amount of media coverage of political activity is an important yardstick to gauge the extent to which political democracy has been realized.

Political news has always consumed a fairly large portion of copy in Chinese newspapers, but the majority of it simply disseminates and implements Party and state policies, laws, and regulations. Few stories cover how such policies, laws, and regulations have been formulated, how feasible they are (whether they conform to social realities and objective laws, and whether they have a strong scientific basis), and whether their formulation has followed democratic principles in accordance with procedures of democratic centralism.

Communication science has identified four types of information in Chinese society: (a) that which promotes decision making, (b) that which instructs, (c) that which manages, and (d) that which creates environment. Of the four, providing information that promotes decision making is the most important function of political news reporting. However, because the media did not function properly for many years, there was no public supervision over decision making in China. People were unable to access valid decision-making information and so could not exercise supervision (through the media) over the formulation of policies, laws, and regulations. They could read about the implementation of government/Party decisions only after the fact, and then the explanation was often one-sided. Nowhere is the detrimental impact of this cycle more clearly illustrated than in the following two events.

First, at the very beginning of the Cultural Revolution, Mao stated that he was in the minority in his support of launching the movement. How then, in a socialist democracy, was the decision made? Did it follow democratic procedures? Why did not the "masters of the society"—the people—have the right to know about it from newspapers? Our media never considered it their duty to report the decision-making process at the highest level. Consequently, even the most antiscientific and antidemocratic of decisions had no chance to be refuted by public opinion. This cycle has continued.

International news reporting by Chinese media in the 1960s and early 1970s was routinely skewed according to the status of a given country's relationship with China. All news from a friendly country was good news, and vice versa. When, in 1969, U.S. astronauts landed on the moon for the first time in human history, the event was reported extensively throughout the world. Live TV coverage alone reached more than 800 million people. In China, however, open-circulation newspapers did not carry a single story about the landing. This is deliberate news bias.

Under the prevailing condition of news bias, how could people draw their own conclusions about international and diplomatic issues? And how could they supervise the "public servants" charged with exercising power on their behalf? Admittedly, international and diplomatic issues are a grave matter, and the press should practice extreme caution to respect China's international relations, but news reporting is not diplomatic announcement. The news media's first responsibility is to satisfy the people's need to learn about major world events. This principle is recognized the world over. So long as we responsibly refrain from couching international news as diplomatic announcement, other countries will not easily take offense.

Practice Objective Reporting

One simple change will take care of many problems. If we are to illuminate heretofore "forbidden areas," expand and invigorate our international news reporting, and change our custom of mixing news reporting with diplomatic announcements, we must promote and practice objective reporting.

All major international events should be fully covered in a timely, objective way, regardless of their outcome or whether or not conclusive judgments are yet available.

This will allow people to learn as the event progresses and so come to a gradual understanding of the nature of things. The Chinese people will be able to know—in the fastest way and to the greatest extent possible—about our turbulent and complicated world, enabling them to better meet the challenges of membership in the international arena.

We have made marked improvements in this regard in recent years. The Chinese news media's reporting of the hostage crisis between the United States and Iran, of the war between Iran and Iraq, and of the workers' strike in Poland was timely, continuous, and objective. The change has won the people's appreciation.

THE FREEDOM TO EXPRESS VIEWS

Freedom of the press naturally includes the freedom to express views and opinions in newspapers. As progress in the production of socialist material goods has provided freer lifestyles for the people, so has the emergence of a modern press ushered in a period of free articulation of their views.

Some people in China have a narrow understanding of speech freedom, maintaining that freedom of speech is limited to the spoken expression of views and does not encompass written articles and newspaper commentary. If that were true, freedom of speech would be nothing more than the freedom to talk. *The Science of the Constitution*, a standard textbook in Chinese universities, clearly defines what is meant: "Freedom of speech refers to citizens' freedom to express their views verbally, in written form or through the medium of their writings as provided for in the Constitution. In a broad sense, therefore, freedom of speech also includes freedom of the press, of publishing, of writing and of painting."[1]

The manifest freedom to express views is critical to socialist press freedom because—although the general public's understanding of the objective world will continue to develop of its own accord—an individual's concepts remain unique. Newspapers have the important task of promoting the societal exchange of those individual perceptions. In that way, the collective understanding will gradually mature and increase in influence. As it does so, erroneous views will tend to diminish. Allowing the free airing of views in newspapers fully conforms to the Marxist theory of knowledge and its method of exploring for truth.

Historical Precedent for the Free Expression of Views

Newspaper publication of proletariat and Party debate is nothing new. Marx and Engels utilized that forum, as did Lenin. When *Spark* was a viable newspaper, Lenin wrote, "Open polemics, conducted in full view of all Russian Social-Democrats and class-conscious workers, is necessary and desirable, and should lead to ideological consensus among Party members."[2] He favored structuring the Party constitution to safeguard the minority's freedoms of speech and press: "We consider it highly important that the arrangements for publication of minority literature—which the Central Committee proposed to the minority of the Second Congress—should be incorporated in the Rules . . . so that the inevitable internal struggles in the Party may be conducted in seemly forms and not allowed to interfere with positive work."

Open discussion through the media would in no way affect uniformity of action. In fact, Lenin regarded free discussion and free criticism as a premise for achieving uniformity of action. More than once, he said, "We have in principle established a definition of the meaning and concept of worker's Party discipline. Uniformity of action, freedom of discussion and freedom of criticism—this is our definition."

The Chinese Communist Party, however, did not inherit this noble tradition. When the proletariat won state power, it should have realized an even stronger guarantee of free discussion and free criticism than before. But those in power feared either that such freedoms would lead to ideological chaos or, if the press were allowed to cover the open Party debate, their reports of the options being considered could be used against the Party.

Under Leftist policy, the intended "uniformity of action . . . freedom of discussion" became "uniformity of action . . . uniformity of opinion." Newspapers were charged with "unifying public opinion." Soon, only the state and certain individuals in power developed policy, and "public criticism and repudiation" replaced free discussion. Newspapers were specifically forbidden to openly discuss political guidelines and policies. It was impossible for people to "consider from various aspects" the positions and policies of the Party and state.

Consequently, the media would applaud the great wisdom of a certain policy one day, and when the next day political lines were reversed, they would repudiate it with equal vigor. The latest set of policies would be unanimously acclaimed. No disagreement whatsoever was allowed. What resulted was a perpetual offensive for "uniformity of opinion." It was precisely these repeated reversals—or "flipping the pancake time and again," in folk language—that ultimately led to ideological chaos among the people [and] provided artillery shells to our enemies.

The Public Opinion Feedback Factor

Judicious policy must be based upon accurate depiction of social practice and objective law. To accomplish this, the citizenry, the Party, and the state must work together. No one group alone can hope to adequately inform effective, considered policy. If newspapers carried the viewpoints of all Party members and of everyone affected by a particular social policy, the exchange would provide the requisite basis for decision making. Public input should also be the catalyst for consistent, constant improvement of existing regulations.

This positive effect of public input on decision making is what I term "the public opinion feedback factor." Although one individual's view can by no means, in and of itself, be assumed to represent truth or provide the sole basis for decision making, still, public deliberation that is fully informed by a complete exchange of views is far more likely to yield increasingly valid, effective policy and law.

Resolving Two Issues from Marx's Theory of Knowledge

Before open dialogue of freely published views can become accepted practice, we need to come to terms with two issues connected with the

Marxist Theory of Knowledge: (1) the plurality of public opinion, and (2) the precept that free speech will not lead to ideological chaos.

The plurality of public opinion

First, we need to recognize the plurality of public opinion and how it applies to different sectors of society. All opinions are not, as some people think, divided only into opposing camps: revolutionary and counterrevolutionary, proletarian and capitalist. Public opinion is inherently pluralistic. Normally, people's opinions vary—some are considered, others fairly one-sided, and still others erroneous. Even the sound ones vary by degree. Each viewpoint has its own rationale, and it is often difficult to judge which opinion is correct.

This plurality benefits a socialist society, because opposing views collectively expressed in the media help society surmount its tendency toward bias or extremism. As purveyors of public opinion, newspapers have the obligation to reflect this plurality, and thus, can optimize its benefit.

But which kind of newspaper content is more desirable: uniformity of public opinion or pluralism? Because of an inconsistency in Mao Zedong's pronouncements on the subject, this issue has long remained unresolved.

In the 1950s, Mao Zedong put forward the policy of "letting a hundred flowers bloom and a hundred schools of thought contend" to address knowledge in the arts and sciences.[3] He advocated cultivating "fragrant flowers" and eradicating "poisonous weeds." Later, however, the words were taken to the extreme, and every intellectual product was soon characterized as either a fragrant flower or a poisonous weed, as if every intellectual product were one or the other. The moment an intellectual product saw the light of day, a label was slapped on it, and either praise or accusation quickly followed. This failure to acknowledge any process toward consensus eventually became a way of thinking, and Mao later pronounced, "We advocate 'letting a hundred schools of thought contend,' and there may be many schools and trends in every branch of learning. But, on the matter of world outlook, there are basically only two contemporary schools, the proletarian and the bourgeois. [The bourgeoisie] must behave itself and is not allowed to be unruly in word or deed."[4]

Why can there not be "a hundred schools" within the proletariat? If we continue to follow the logic of Mao's last "only two schools" theory, people of the proletarian class can express only the sponsored viewpoint, and whoever expresses a divergent opinion is spreading bourgeois propaganda. This is obviously absurd.

Today, we must free ourselves from this chaos. To continue the metaphor, in the natural world, there exist flowers that are not fragrant and weeds that are not poisonous. Yet each has its own value. Certainly, along the continuum of viewpoints and intellectual products on a certain subject, there can be found "fragrant flowers" and "poisonous weeds." More commonly, however, an intellectual product will be sound, for the most part, but contain some errors. Likewise, an erroneous viewpoint can still contain rational, positive elements. It is, therefore, neither appropriate to categorically laud something as a "fragrant flower" and forbid any challenge to its precepts, nor proper to denigrate something as a "poisonous weed" and summarily ban it. Only by allowing the free expression of different views and by continual analysis and quality comparison can people create a thriving environment within which worthwhile intellectual products flourish.

The free airing of views does not lead to ideological chaos

There is no need to be overly concerned that open discussion of views will lead to ideological chaos. Postrevolutionary journalism theories have long held that "every word and every article of a newspaper should and must represent the thinking of the Party."[5] Because newspapers have virtually abandoned their function as purveyors of public opinion, China's people think of newspapers as tools of the ruling party and state power.

After decades of "two schools" theories, the free airing of subjective views in the media might seem as though it would produce a chaos of diverse thoughts. But if we actually carry out press reforms and then make clear the news media's true role, people will become accustomed to the free airing of views in the media, and the so-called "chaos of diversity" will be regarded as ideological liveliness. As a matter of fact, with the development of political democracy in China, the Chinese people are already becoming accustomed to—and welcoming—the reflection of all kinds of views in the news media.

This pattern of progress has already been established. In 1956, individuals who were vehemently opposed to open media discussion of "whether Chinese schools should adopt the USSR's physical training program" said discussion would adversely affect program implementation and could even cause negative side effects. Today, nobody would be worried about open discussion of such trivial matters.

These days, newspapers extensively discuss major reform issues such as economic reform and reform of the cadre system. When the media carried many speeches of deputies to the Fifth National People's Congress at its 1980 Third Plenary Session, criticisms, suggestions, and proposals filled page after newspaper page. This had been unthinkable in the past, yet, instead of causing confusion, the practice received genuine popular appreciation, nationwide.

It is ignorance that breeds alarm. The more often people come into contact with different views, the calmer they will remain when the unexpected happens. As long ago as 1906, reformer and journalist Liang Qichao said in his "Letter to My Colleagues,"

Newspapers may get a bit extreme in their views, but that is not a problem. Why not? If I am extreme at this end, inevitably someone is being extreme at the other end, and then there will be another person who takes the middle road. Taken together, they yield to, correct, and inform one another. Truth is sure to be born from this. If, on the other hand, people follow one another in expressing the same vague ideas, the whole nation might be perfectly calm and tranquil in mental activities, but national progress in every field would stop.

Twenty years ago, many people were shocked to hear about Western culture, but when the fearsome idea of political reform emerged, their fear of Western culture was replaced by dread of reform. . . . Then, when years later, the idea of civil rights for the people emerged, their fear of political reform was supplanted by fear of civil rights. As soon as the idea of a revolution emerged, their fear of civil rights was obliterated by fear of revolution.

In the intellectual circles of China today, probably only one in a thousand is not afraid of a revolution; one in a hundred is unafraid of the idea of civil rights for the people; as for political reform and Western culture, fear is totally gone.[6]

Liang's reasoning in 1906 remains valid today: that which is at first startling can become commonplace. Precisely for that reason, the appearance in the news media of differing opinions—or even extreme views—is no cause for concern. Our leaders and the people are more broad-minded than before. There is an atmosphere of political democracy in the country. We have moved into an atmosphere for press freedom.

THE FREEDOM TO CRITICIZE

Newspaper commentary the world over is leveled at three elements of society: (1) those in power, including the government and its officials; (2) unscrupulous people, deeds, and phenomena; and (3) concepts of a theoretical nature.

The Chinese media have generally had no problem with the latter two, but the issue of the socialist news media's freedom to criticize the government and its officials is as yet unresolved, both in theory and in practice. Even so, because this type of criticism is essential for the proletariate to intelligently function, the socialist news media must embrace it.[7]

Theory supports social masters criticizing social servants; the people have the right to criticize the Party and the government. The Constitution specifically stipulates, "Citizens of the People's Republic of China have the right to criticize and offer suggestions to all government organs and officials."[8] In the field of journalism, however, not even theoretical studies have broached the issue of the Chinese citizen's right to criticize and exercise supervision over the government through the news media.

In 1945 Yan'an,[9] Mao Zedong received Huang Yanpei, a progressive. Huang commented that Chinese history has moved in constant cycles of instability, as evidenced in families, organizations, and dynasties. "When you Communists gain state power in the future," he asked Mao, "how are you going to break out of this cycle?"

Mao answered that we found a new way to break this cycle and this new way would be democracy. "Only by letting people supervise the government can the government remain effective," Mao said. "Only when every person has the initiative to care about state affairs can a government endure."

Government Supervision by Public Opinion

Mao Zedong regarded the people's supervision of government as the means to government stability. Four key components of that supervision included (a) legislation, (b) convening the People's Congress, (c) elections, and (d) the system for removing officials. There is a fifth.

A fifth and critical component is supervision by public opinion, which possesses attributes not found in the other four. For example, the People's Congress—the most deliberative of the four supervisory components—is convened only at scheduled times and can consider only those issues for which it has time, whereas supervision by public opinion is constant.

Until the proletariat had political power and its party had become the ruling one, there was less urgent need for supervision from public opinion. During the period of democratic revolution, the Party looked to reaction in the press to discover and correct its mistakes. Because the Party was daily encircled by an armed enemy and attacked in that enemy's reactionary press, it could not afford to be divorced from the people even for a single day. Any fundamental error in policy would quickly manifest itself in shrinking Party ranks, reduction of the political base, or even failure of the revolution. As a result, misguided political direction was usually corrected quickly.

After the Party became the country's ruling party—especially after political power had been consolidated—it was considerably more difficult to discover possible mistakes of the Party's own making. It was even more difficult to correct them. To accomplish that, the Party would have had to adjust its policies in the press, develop supervision by public opinion, and listen to views different from its own. Because the government chose not to do that, it was possible for the Great Leap Forward's national boasting chorus of 1958 to continue unabated until the spring of 1960. It is also why, during the Cultural Revolution, the popular will could be suppressed for as long as ten years.

A socialist press should have the associated right of supervision through the free publishing of public opinion. Inherent in this provision is the right of the people to criticize the government and its officials through the news media, within the bounds allowed by the Constitution and other laws. The Party press should also abide by the Party Constitution and its resolutions.

On this basis, the press should have the freedom to criticize whatever and whomever it thinks deserves criticism, without seeking prior approval from anyone. Prior approval of commentary had been mandatory for a long time. When people want to criticize their "public representatives" through the news media, approval must come from the very "representatives" they criticize.[10]

It is precisely this theory and system that so ably served Lin Biao and the Gang of Four. They committed countless crimes against the people, but because they were the pinnacles of state power, the press could never hope to gain approval to criticize them. Feng Yingzi, a veteran journalist, masterfully dissected this issue in his article titled "On Miss Kung's Dog and Jiang Qing's Horses."

When Japan . . . escalated its war in the Pacific, the second daughter of H. H. Kung (the finance minister of China's Kuomintang government), [luxuriously] flew from Hong Kong to the Chinese war capital of Chongqing, with her dog in tow. Public opinion in Chongqing was outraged, and so was national public opinion. Even newspapers financed by her father joined the lambasting. Decades later, when Mao Zedong was seriously ill, his wife Jiang Qing had the impudence to tour Daizhai Village in Shaanxi province by special train, taking with her four horses and courtiers great and small. This was more outrageous than Miss Kung's behavior, but as long as Jiang Qing held power, her scandalous behavior would remain hidden from the public.[11]

Because it was during the Kuomintang period, Miss Kung's lambasting in the puppet press must be considered little more than bogus, bourgeoisie democracy. But it did give people an idea of how the rich and the powerful lived, and it did compel Miss Kung and her ilk to adopt some scruples. And yet, our own socialist papers could not expose the scandalous behavior of Jiang Qing.

This can lead to only one conclusion: our journalistic system does not meet the standards of a country aspiring to a high degree of democracy. "Were there a morsel of democracy, even the kind of superficial democracy used to expose Miss Kung, there would have been no breeding ground for the Gang of Four."[12]

The Current State of "Approved Criticisms"

Those criticisms that survive the approval process are often belated. Not until after Lin Biao's downfall was it finally reported that he had spent large sums of foreign currency to build a luxurious house, one in which a single bed cost hundreds of thousands of yuan. Only after the Gang of Four's collapse was it finally reported that gang member Yao Wenyuan had been living in more than 100 rooms of a middle school, having renovated them as his private residence by creating a luxurious interior within an ordinary exterior. Not until the Third Plenary Session of the eleventh National Congress of the Party had already convened in 1978 could newspapers report that this former Party propaganda leader had spent seven million yuan building the residence for himself and his daughter. The list of instances like these is endless.

No matter how compelling the justification for delaying these reports, the people would still be justified in asking why the press was not allowed to expose such criminal extravagance in a timely manner. Had a system of socialist and democratic media been able to guarantee that our social servants were subject to public opinion supervision, including how they perform their official duties and what kind of official benefits they receive, these people would not have dared to acquire such luxurious houses.

Even with regard to exposure of criminals and wrongdoing at lower levels, "approved" criticism is about as effective as "mending the fence after the sheep is lost." There is no chance to limit damage with a timely response, since it is difficult for members of the approving organization to reach consensus on the need to permit public exposure. Only when the problems have developed to a very serious degree is such consensus reached quickly.

Most "approved" criticisms do not see the light of day while problems are developing. Rather, they either come on the heels of events, when conclusions are already being drawn and penalties meted out, or after losses have already been suffered.

Freedom to Criticize as the Best Solution

Freedom to offer open commentary not only fosters a sense of responsibility in the press, it also allows flexibility as to the most appropriate means of criticism. In cases where the ramifications of an emerging issue are still unclear, or if criticism would be inappropriate for good reason, the press may best serve the people not by running a critical report or commentary, but by objectively reporting all facets of the story. Such timely, objective reporting would serve all concerned by alerting the individuals who directly impact the issue and by informing the judgment of the general readership. In this way, significant damage would be prevented or at least contained.

The responsible criticism of issues and individuals certainly demands consideration and caution. Concerted effort should be made to ensure that media analyses benefit the people and the Party. Leveling irresponsible criticism is an abuse of press power. It is both wrong and counterproductive. These articles must demonstrate absolute respect for fact. The standard of timely coverage should not preclude thorough research and confirmation of all facts. In cases where published criticism proves to be unfounded, the press should make self-criticisms and carry corrections.

In summary, I do not favor a system requiring "pre-approval" for press criticism, but propose a system in which the press solicits, on its own initiative, input from relevant governmental departments and individuals. This will not only ensure the accuracy of the criticisms but will accelerate resolution of the issues addressed.

FREEDOM TO PUBLISH NEWSPAPERS

The bourgeois[13] idea of "freedom to publish newspapers" is actually freedom to use capital to compete freely in the business of publishing. Large corporations run the vast majority of influential publications in capitalist countries, whereas the laboring class can afford to publish only small publications.

According to Marx, the primary freedom of the press lies in not making a profit. Only in socialist countries, where the people have gained political power and taken possession of the means of production, is newspaper publishing free of competition to see who can spend the most money—free of the confines of a trade's focus on profit. Freedom to publish newspapers under a socialist system involves the development of a multi-tiered, socialist newspaper business that can better safeguard and develop the socialist economic base and promote socialist democracy. To move deliberately toward such a model, we must understand the past and then move beyond it.

The Evolution of Our Current Press Model

In the brief period immediately following the founding of new China, the press had a new lease on life. For a time, Party and non-Party newspapers coexisted with non-Party publications. Together, state-owned newspapers, state and public sector papers,[14] joint-ownership publications, and private ownership papers flourished.

However, under the rapidly encroaching influence of the Soviet model, the non-Party newspapers became increasingly scarce, and both private business publications and those of the various democratic parties soon disappeared all together. The ensuing Soviet-modeled press structure was made up almost entirely of publications put out by official Party echelon committees.

Next, the State Press and Publications Administration—originally established to oversee the press—was abolished, its functions assigned to propaganda departments of various Party committees.

By 1967–69, only forty-two newspapers and twenty periodicals remained in this vast country. The news media was ripe to become both perpetrator and victim of the Cultural Revolution.

During the thirty years from 1949 to 1979, press development noticeably lagged behind that of other sectors in China's new society. Not until the fall of the Gang of Four did China's press experience rapid recovery and development.

That model remains largely intact. Currently,[15] all newspapers are organs of Party committees at different levels, except for the few published by national organizations such as the trade unions and the Communist Youth League. The majority of daily papers are political, their main function to provide directives on specific kinds of work. The national newspapers rarely transcend the administrative boundaries within which they are published, and all papers look basically alike. This is not surprising.

Moving Beyond the Past

Although this problem is due, in part, to economic backwardness and a generally low educational level, it is also the result of a problematic journalistic system. The highly centralized political system begot a highly centralized news and publishing system, which, in turn, restricted initiative in newspaper publishing.

We are in this state of affairs because we continue to blindly adhere to custom instead of carrying out the reform necessary to meet the new challenges of new circumstances.

It must be said that the model we cling to was originally a sound one. During the period of democratic revolution, our central task was to engage in a revolutionary war. All our efforts in the economic and cultural development sectors, central to the revolution, were aimed at ensuring its success. This called for unified Party leadership. It would have been counterproductive to decentralize the message with Party-run, government-run, and public-run newspapers. Consequently, there was one Party paper at the central level and one Party paper for each revolutionary base and administrative region.

But now the revolution is over, and under socialist economic market conditions, there should be a considerable change in this practice. An atmosphere of progress calls for a wide variety of publications, some of them run by the Party, some by the government, and some privately run. An effectual press model must encourage vigorous, diverse publications of varied content and writing styles, even as it upholds Party leadership and the socialist system and abides by the Constitution and other laws.

Diversity in our publications would serve the diverse needs of the public. One newspaper might target government workers; another, ordinary people. Some magazines might target educated readers; others, those with only a primary education. Specialized publications could be published for distinct occupations. Some readers might prefer a combination of news and commentary; others would prefer to read primarily news. Some papers could traverse administrative districts.

Party and government entities have an important role to play in a socialist newspaper structure. In Western journalism theories, governments and ruling parties may not interfere in news reporting, which is considered an encroachment on the freedom of the press. This theory is not suited to the socialist system.

The purpose of political democracy and press freedom is to provide a means to promote social justice, social fairness, and social progress. Neither the political structure nor the press exists for its own sake. The government and the ruling party are composed of the socially informed elite. As part of a tiered system of information sources, their publications would serve to explain resolutions to the people, enhance political efficiency, and achieve social developmental objectives. Politics in this system is a threat only when (*a*) no newspapers exist except those of the ruling party and the government, (*b*) when the ruling party and the government monopolize sources of information, and (*c*) when they monopolize interpretation of a nation's political process.

At the other extreme, if all the news media in a country are privately owned, the system will inevitably become completely commercialized. Their search for profits will lead them to yellow journalism, rendering a free press uncivilized and unhealthy.

If a country has a sufficient number of government-run and Party newspapers—with hard news constituting the bulk of the coverage— their positive influence will outweigh any negative impact. Yellow journalism will be held in check, the trend toward commercialization will be stopped, and social ethics will be improved.

Establish Non-Party Newspapers

I believe that we need to launch new newspapers, and, at the same time, improve the quality of Party newspapers. In 1956, Liu Shaoqi[16] proposed that the official New China News Agency start "a news-oriented paper which can openly declare its intention to compete against

The People's Daily." His proposal never got off the ground. Some members of the leadership were concerned that a second government-run newspaper would be suspected of "creating more than one [political] center," which would hamper unified leadership.

We have long understood in our ongoing efforts to improve and strengthen Party leadership that it is problematic to separate the functions of the Party and the government and then let the Party run everything. Such misplaced emphasis encourages the Party to appropriate certain government functions, weakens the people's democracy, and harms Party leadership itself. Yet, because of excessive emphasis on the media's uniqueness, this counterproductive practice has been the very one used to manage the news media sector.

It is high time to establish the policy that all levels of government may publish newspapers as long as there is a need and conditions permit. Party and government newspapers might have different emphases, with Party papers primarily directed to cadres and Party members, and government papers primarily serving ordinary people. According to that same principle, the people's provincial and municipal congresses and the various committees of the Chinese People's Political Consultative Conference should also be allowed to publish their own papers. The same treatment should be given to existing democratic parties, which are political alliances of patriots serving socialism under the leadership of the Communist Party.

A socialist press should also have "min-ban" (publicly run) newspapers and periodicals. Party and government news organs are run by "representatives" on behalf of the people, whereas min-ban newspapers are those that are run directly by the people.

There is no reason to presuppose that different organizations running their own separate newspapers will affect dramatic differences in content. That fear has held us back in the past.

In 1957, when some people floated the idea of starting "tong-ren" newspapers (those run by colleagues), they were accused of "putting on a rival show against the Party."[17] To be accurate, tong-ren newspapers was simply the term used to distinguish those publications from official papers. The form is one under which people could directly exercise their rights to freedom of speech and freedom of the press, and within which they could—through choice—directly regulate the quality and quantity of news and information transmitted by the media. Without question, it complements the existing media structure, providing a venue through which people work together of their own free will to enjoy the right of press freedom within the bounds provided by the Constitution and other laws.

Lenin strongly and repeatedly advocated publicly run, freely published newspapers. "The government of the workers' and peasants' asserts that freedom of the press constitutes (a) freeing the press from control by capital, (b) transferring paper mills and printing houses to state property, and (c) allowing every citizen group with a certain enrollment [10,000 members, for example] to enjoy the right to a corresponding amount of paper and a corresponding amount of printing labor."

Lenin also pointed out that in a fair distribution of paper and printing labor, the government should also give a proportionate share to minor parties, to any citizen group with a certain number of members, or to those having collected a certain number of signatures. Although the environment of the times prevented the realization of Lenin's concept, Lenin's statements show that, at least in theory, min-ban or tong-ren newspapers have a place in socialist society.

At the third sessions of the Fifth National People's Congress and the Fifth National Committee of the Chinese People's Political Consultative Conference (CPPCC), convened in 1980, many deputies and committee members raised the issue of guaranteeing citizens freedom of the press. Committee member Li Ziyong said, "Let all citizens of the country have the freedom to openly express their views and publish newspapers and periodicals."

Su Xin, another committee member, said, "On the premise of abiding by the 'Four Cardinal Principles'[18]—adherence to Party leadership being at their core—we should allow individuals to have the right to publish books, start newspapers and periodicals, and run printing houses." Evidently, public demand is considerable for allowing publication of min-ban (publicly run) newspapers.

The Four Features of Min-Ban Newspapers

Min-ban newspapers are indispensable in a socialist society because they have features that are absent in their official counterparts.

Supplementing the official press

First, a min-ban press serves as a supplement to the official press. As such, it offers an effective means by which to encourage the free airing of views and to enliven an atmosphere of democracy. If those in power deviate from truth and democracy, the min-ban press can—by exercising its rights as prescribed by law and precedent—bring to light the imprudent aspects of a given plan or practice. In this way, min-ban publications can be the voice of the people and put to an end a situation in which public opinion is completely suppressed.

Less influence than official publications

Second, since any given min-ban publication expresses the viewpoint of only part of the populous, it has less authority and less influence than its official counterpart. Therefore, it should have more freedom in the expression of opinions. This greater freedom would, in turn, promote a higher quality of discussion and hence, better solutions.

Some people liken the min-ban press to a small experimental plot of land and its official counterpart to large tracts of farming fields. Once the official press takes full advantage of the input offered by the min-ban press, their published policies will be more fully informed. The citizenry will notice the inevitable improvement in their lives and in the country. And the min-ban press—having proven itself to be of benefit to society—will call upon the official press for access to confirmation by credible sources, thus creating an environment of accuracy, objectively informed commentary, and optimum benefit to China and her people.

Reflects a wide range of viewpoints

The third feature of the min-ban press is that it can cover a wider range of viewpoints. On international and diplomatic issues, it can serve the government by providing a spectrum of public opinion. Li Chunqing, a member of the CPPCC National Committee, said, "When it is necessary, unofficial public organizations should openly express their views on major national issues. [The unofficial press] should participate in international debates by carrying the views of parties, groups and individuals. The diversity in perspectives and recommendations should be allowed to form 'an orchestra of voices' under the leadership of the Communist Party."[19]

Cultivates new workers

Fourth, the min-ban press can function much the same as a cultivating garden does. The min-ban press can be a source for nurturing new reporters, commentators, and writers.

HOW TO CREATE A MIN-BAN PRESS

It is time to explore—under socialist conditions—specific ways to develop China's min-ban press. It seems appropriate to require, through legislation, that within a given time frame, each city with a population of more than 1 million may have one or two min-ban newspapers. Such newspapers may or may not be privately owned.

Publishers of min-ban papers could be recommended by a "press evaluation committee," composed, by thirds, of government officials, journalists, and people from social circles unrelated to either the government or the press. When each member's term of office ends, the committee could suggest renewal or recommend other candidates. This will lead to both quantitative and qualitative standardization of the min-ban press.

The coexistence of Party and min-ban newspapers calls for the establishment of two administrative criteria: the constitutional criterion and the Party criterion. Party newspapers should abide by both whereas the min-ban press need abide only by the constitutional criterion (including laws enacted in accordance with the Constitution, of course). The two criteria have a common basis: adherence to the Four Cardinal Principles.

The constitutional criterion would be set at a basic level: the press shall be protected and not be subject to government restrictions, as long as it does not violate the Constitution or special laws enacted in accordance with the Constitution. By comparison, the Party criterion would require that Party papers, in addition to abiding by laws, follow the Party's guidance in matters of principle and reflect the Party's policy thinking.

An Orchestra of Voices

The coexistence of a Party press and a min-ban press will result in a condition of socialist press freedom in which "an orchestra of voices" has both a clear main theme and a rich harmony.

NOTES

1. *Selected Works of Marx and Engels*, vol. 2, p. 441, The People's Press, 1972.

2. Lenin first published *The Spark* (*Iskra*) in December 1900, from Stuttgart.

3. Mao launched the Hundred Flowers Movement in 1956. Scholars have debated whether the movement was a cynical ploy to expose anti-Party sentiment among intellectuals or whether the breadth and virulence of the criticism that had surfaced genuinely surprised Mao by May 1957. In any event, the movement ended abruptly in mid-1957, and many of the intellectuals who had spoken out became targets of the Anti-Rightist Campaign of June 1957.

4. *Selected Works of Mao Zedong*, vol. 5, p. 407, The People's Press, (1977).

5. The Collection of Chinese Communist Party Documents on Journalistic Work.

6. Liang Qichao was a leading intellectual of the late Qing dynasty, an advocate of enlightened autocracy.

7. Press criticism includes not only commentaries and editorials that challenge policy, but articles that provide a viewpoint different from that of the government and/or Party position as well as those that present new facts.

8. Article 41, Constitution of 1982.

9. Mao's headquarters from the end of the Long March in 1935 until the end of World War II in 1945.

10. The quotation marks are Sun's.

11. *Xinhua Monthly Digest*, 2nd issue, The People's Press, 1980.

12. Editor's note—Sun is saying that a freer media will take responsibility for the integrity of its reporting, even to the point of admitting fault and printing retractions when appropriate. Again, the process Sun proposes is a very simple one in the West. In China, however, he must painstakingly offer a plausible argument to explain this. He does so in the terminology of the historic form of public criticism: denouncement and public self-criticism.

13. "Bourgeois" can be read "capitalist."

14. Editor's note—The term "public sector" here is not what is meant in the West. State, government, and Party publications originate from official departments, whereas public sector–run publications would originate from the perceived need and efforts of ordinary citizens who, in turn, would publish through printing centers ("means of publication") provided by the Constitution. These public sector entities, however, still operate under the auspices of their government departments.

15. Early 1980s.

16. Liu Shaoqi was Mao's longtime comrade and chief of state until he was denounced during the Cultural Revolution.

17. Tong-ren and min-ban newspapers are essentially the same concept. Tong-ren is the older term, coined by journalists who wanted to start their own papers with colleagues. Min-ban means "run by the people." They are the same press structure.

18. Deng Xiaoping coined these guiding statements in a speech given March 30, 1979: "We must keep to the socialist road. We must uphold the dictatorship of the proletariat. We must uphold the leadership of the Communist Party. We must uphold Marxism-Leninism and Mao Zedong thought."

19. This support provided the environment in which Sun could begin to publish his theories.

CHAPTER 4 _____

Press Freedom Is a Process

PRESS FREEDOM IS NOT STATIC

We have discussed from different perspectives the necessity for and feasibility of socialist press freedom. However, simply believing that press freedom is necessary for China and feasible does not make it materialize. Like socialism, press freedom is not static, but a process that continuously develops in compliance with its nature and according to the conditions provided by history.

Press freedom follows the same trends that govern the development of civilization. The extent to which we are socialized and, particularly, the extent to which a society produces materials, determine the extent and nature of all freedoms of humanity. This is also true of press freedom, which differs widely in societies with different rates of production.

Today, we champion a people's democratic dictatorship,[1] a system whose ultimate purpose is to nurture a society in which, as Karl Marx said, "The free development of each is the condition for the free development of all." The process of realizing a people's democratic dictatorship, therefore, should and must be marked by ever-increasing press freedom. At every stage of socialism, press freedom should advance.

Press freedom must also develop in tandem with technological progress. Consider the relationship between national politics and technology. When, in 1772, a Philadelphia newspaper reported an event that had happened in England only thirty-five days earlier, its timeliness created quite a sensation. By 1981, news of an assassination attempt on then U.S. President Ronald Reagan reached every American home through radio and TV broadcasts within seven minutes.[2]

In the last decade, technological dissemination of news has become the rule throughout the world. Increased press freedom must proceed in tandem with that material and technological progress. The country that ignores or blocks this trend will lose in the global competition for information. Isolation is not a viable option.

PRESS FREEDOM IS NOT FINITE

Press freedom is not a finite line; it is a ray of light without end. A clear understanding of how press freedom unfolds with society will help us conceptualize the conditions for its development. This must be clearly established if we are to prevent socialist press freedom from being curtailed yet again. This is a critical objective of our study.

It is clear from the above analysis that we cannot hope to suddenly awake on some bright morning to find press freedom in place, full blown and thriving. At different stages of socialism, press freedom will take its form from the conditions prepared in the preceding stage. Marx reflected on this process: "Men make history, but they do not make it just as they please; they do not make it under circumstances chosen by themselves, but under circumstances directly encountered, given and transmitted from the past."

In China, "circumstances transmitted from the past" were rather backward. It is difficult to develop press freedom in an environment of strong feudal customs and habits. Many of the calamities that befell the Chinese media during the Cultural Revolution were the result of a retaliation of feudalism against socialist democracy. But feudalism is not the only enemy of press freedom in China.

The forces of anarchism and liberalism, products themselves of feudalism, continue to actively resist a socialist press. Therefore, in striving for socialist press freedom, we have to fight on two fronts: Press freedom must keep step, first, with China's modernization, and second, with the country's democratization through the rule of law.

PRESS FREEDOM SHOULD DEVELOP IN SYNC WITH CHINA'S MODERNIZATION PROGRAM

Political Stability Is a Prerequisite to Successful Modernization

There will not be political stability without political democratization that includes press freedom. However, press reform that seeks to quickly achieve a high level of freedom without regard for the country's current economic and educational conditions would be more than foolhardy; it would be harmful.

China's economic reform has achieved remarkable success, but we still face a backward economy and a host of challenges. An illustration will serve to explain China's dilemma. One reform objective is to ultimately move beyond our system of power centralization. To accomplish that reform, however, we will temporarily need centralization of power. We must make use of and maintain the current system in order to change it. Even so, political democracy will inevitably expand, and a free press and economic development will consequentially follow.

Press Freedom Develops in Sync with Political Democratization and the Establishment of a Functioning Legal System

The countries that benefit from press freedom are those run by the rule of law. Effective order can be maintained only when freedom is checked by laws. Such is the case in Japan, where the constitution gives the media the freedoms of reporting and commentary, including the freedom to criticize government bans. Even so, the criticism does not undermine the bans in the least; violators cannot hope to escape punishment until such time as the bans are legally repealed.

China needs the same system: press freedom and a clear-cut legal structure. However, the Chinese legal system is still immature. The authority of law must be increased, and the public must be made aware of the law.

The way things are at present, newspaper articles can both facilitate and undermine law enforcement. Some time ago, an article discussed whether or not "transporting goods from one place to another for the purpose of sale" constituted "engaging in speculation and profiteering." Apparently, the article led both citizens and law enforcement officials to ignore the law as invalid. In this case, the newspaper article superseded Chinese "law." This could happen for two reasons: (a) the long-standing organizational mouthpiece role of the press that perpetuated the "managing of state affairs by means of newspapers and editorials," and (b) our failure to establish the rule of law in its true sense.

There is a comparatively straightforward explanation as to why the rule of law has been difficult to establish. In the 1940s, Party-led revolutionary activities involved breaking Koumintang law, causing a rapid decline in regard for any laws. After the founding of new China, the Party's mass movements did not proceed in accordance with defined law. This further eroded the authority of the law among the populace, culminating in utter lawlessness in the decade of the Cultural Revolution.

THE TASK AHEAD

Today, we are striving to institute a socialist legal system. Creating the system is, in and of itself, a lengthy process of writing legislation, promoting public respect, and deciding on appropriate enforcement. But our task goes far beyond enacting laws to guide our society. Before laws can be followed and enforced, we must first accomplish the more arduous task of purposefully countermanding the influence of the "arbitrary rule of man." Development of press freedom must proceed in sync with a national legal system.

We should have high-minded long-term goals for press freedom that spring from realistic initial strategies. Even initial reform will require daring leadership and public support. Of vital importance is initiative from journalists themselves. They must purposefully do their jobs according to the rules of their profession, instead of passively waiting for something nice to happen.

Journalists' initiatives have proven to make a positive difference. The Central Television Station produced a live broadcast of the trial of the Gang of Four, and the papers printed in full the charges brought against them by the deputies of the National People's Congress. This coverage happened because journalists, in direct response to public demand, actively pursued endorsement of the programs in question.

That a lively press will inevitably trigger some problems is no reason to unequivocally deny the greater benefit. Economic reform and the ensuing lively economy have also triggered problems. Zhao Ziyang, the former general secretary of the CCP observed, "We should not panic, hesitate or retreat at the first sign of trouble. On the contrary, we should study and analyze things, guiding our actions according to circumstances, and thereby find timely solutions to the problems that will inevitably arise in our march toward a better future."[3]

Development of socialist press freedom is unstoppable. The advent of political democratization and press freedom in China is irresistible.

NOTES

1. In this system, the people "dictate" through a democratic process.

2. This would have been new information to Sun's audience. When this article was first published, the timeliness of the report on Reagan would have been impossible in China.

3. *The People's Daily*, April 21, 1980, p. 1.

Personal Opinions on Macro-Issues in Press Reform

The following article was published in the ninth issue of the 1984 *Journalism Institute Newsletter*. It represents the first article since the founding of the People's Republic that discusses the broad policy issue of press reform in China. Although these proposals ultimately predicted the ensuing reforms, this was the first time these views had been proposed. Publication was quite difficult, and many of the proposals were censored several times after they were first published. Over the years, most of the author's suggestions have been either borne out in practice or fully adopted. In 1996, the author added several contemporary examples.

Chinese journalism reached a zenith after the 1978 Third Plenum of the Eleventh Party Congress.[1] Due in part to wise and sound policies formulated by the Party, the upswing was also the result of the active, creative efforts of journalists who realized their responsibility to both the Party and the people, thereby moving gradually but deliberately toward press reform.

The demand for a free press emerged in press circles as early as 1979. It emerged at a time when China was criticizing the cultural autocracy and pretentious writing style of the Gang of Four, demanding the return to a more practical, realistic tradition and a livelier writing mode. Since then, journalism has made notable progress in timeliness, freshness, quantity, and brevity. Criticism has enjoyed a pronounced increase in prestige and effectiveness.

Readership demand has also become a major concern. Certain press entities have conducted large-scale surveys on reader preferences, interests, and needs. These surveys have allowed them to markedly improve both readability and service. Journalists have also become active participants in the community through charities and organized events, thus broadening their relationship with the wider audience. Compared with the structures that had been in place, these achievements are dramatic.

PRESS REFORMS NEED INFORMED PUBLIC INPUT

Although these press reforms have produced immediate and tangible results, most of them have dealt strictly with outward style and format. The timely, fresh news of late has been the journalistic standard ever since the Yan'an period.[2] Although journalists should have been obligated to that standard all along, reestablishing it through our current efforts is indeed progress.

Although we should take pride in the recent reforms, we should not overrate them. The pace has not been fast enough.

Design a General Plan for Reform

First, we have lacked an overall plan for reform. By that, I mean a clear and reasonably unified conceptualization of the mission, prerequisites, starting point, and conditions necessary for reform. Of course, press reform primarily depends upon journalistic integrity and the bold creativity and innovation of the comrades who will be involved in the practical work of reform itself. It is therefore impossible to design every detail in advance. But without initial, deliberate discussion of an overall plan, the result will surely be a watered-down proposal that will effect little more than perfunctory reform.

Reform Must Be Expedited

Second, the pace of reform has been too slow because public opinion has been uninformed. Mental and theoretical preparation has been inadequate. Because there has been neither open research nor discussion conceptualizing the factors involved in press reform, society has insufficient understanding of journalism work, of the rules that journalism must follow, or of the potential of the socialist press industry. Thus, it is difficult for press reform to gain momentum from public opinion.

Moreover, many journalists themselves have no concept of the prospects for reform because of lingering Leftist ideas that limit their thought.

Correcting this situation will certainly depend upon a sense of urgency from appropriate government and Party leaders, but I think press circles should consciously promote change themselves. There are several hundred thousand journalists at newspapers, news agencies, broadcasting stations, and television stations across the country. They have the nation's ear on a daily basis. They should endorse, defend, and spread journalistic research and reform. The most outstanding talents in the field, especially those courageous reformers pioneering new territory, should speak out on the subject with force and with righteousness.

All of the recent economic reforms have been accompanied by deep, ongoing discussion of economic theory. That discussion has, in turn, generated informed public opinion and support for economic reform. Although press reform could not be handled on the same scale, the work would be much easier if press reform had just one-hundredth or one-thousandth of the public interest accorded economic reform.

EMPHASIS SHOULD BE ON REFORM OF MACRO-ISSUES

Just like economic reform, press reform has macro-and micro-issues. The day-to-day reforms should be regarded as micro-issue reform. For example, many comrades believe that the decision to cover a meeting should be determined by the meeting's news value and no longer depend on political protocol or the level of leaders who attend. They think that published interviews and reports from the meeting should provide valuable information to the public. Various press units have recently been concerned with such micro-issues. If they can be resolved satisfactorily, they will represent important reforms that can quickly accumulate.

Macro-issue reform refers mainly to reform of the press system itself, its policy, its administrative mechanism, and the industry's structure. It also includes reform of the professional fields that affect the discipline of journalism. These reforms happen beyond the printed page, but will ultimately be manifest there.

Macro-issue reforms are deeper and more profound than micro-issue reforms. Traditionally, discussion of macro-issues in press reform is rare. It has not appeared in public media, and, in fact, the subject is barely mentioned even in the internal media of various press units.

Why should we initiate macro-issue press reform? I think the fundamental reason is the dramatic difference between our present society and that of the revolutionary times in which China's Party newspaper policy was designed.

Few entities have remained as they were at the beginning of the revolution. From the Party's position to the Party's priorities, from the people's cultural level to their level of awareness, all differ dramatically from that of revolutionary times. In the same way, the function of the press industry should be different, if not in essence, then in diversity.

As a case in point, public input has not been emphasized for thirty years. When the Communist Party was still oppressed, any errors in strategy and policy or any actions that contradicted the will of the masses always and immediately resulted in the reduction of the revolutionary team, the deterioration of revolutionary bases, or in failure of the movement itself. During revolutionary times, an unsound social strategy might persist for as long as three years, but unsound policy could never have lasted the ten years or more that the Cultural Revolution would some twenty years later. In the early years, the Party did not require formalized supervision by public opinion to discover and correct errors.

Once it became the ruling party, however, and especially after political power was consolidated, the Party needed to develop reliable channels for public supervision of its effectiveness. The Party needed to understand the wishes and requirements of the masses, to prevent and quickly correct errors, and to avail itself of the people's intelligence so that informed decisions could be made concerning the country's stability and prosperity. To develop this kind of effective public supervision today, we must concentrate on adhering to the sound traditions of Party newspaper policy and developing appropriate new strategies.

The recent history of China's press—particularly the bitter lesson of the Cultural Revolution when the people's voice was suppressed—should be proof enough that reform is needed. Not only must we re-emphasize the socialist character of the press and the tenet that the proletariat should control the mass media, but we must also recognize and adjust the system according to the theoretical realities of the press itself. Without fully examining the latter, we cannot achieve the former. And to accomplish that, we must base the press system upon socialist democracy and legality and so guarantee the rights and obligation of mass media to act according to the Constitution and constitutionally based laws. Press legislation is now on the national agenda, and Party authority over the press can be openly discussed, as can the practice of governing the press by law.

REFORM SUGGESTIONS FOR FIVE MACRO-ISSUES

The macro-issues in press reform provide a limitless wellspring for discussion and change. This discussion will concentrate on five of those macro-issues: (1) developing a tri-level press; (2) revising news format; (3) managing newspapers as enterprises; (4) refining the administrative mechanism; and (5) augmenting the press's guidance function to include social practice.

Macro-Issue 1—Developing a Tri-level Press Structure with Party Newspapers, Official Newspapers, and Nonofficial Newspapers

In some ways, China's newspaper structure is already multi-layered. There are newspapers published specifically for workers, peasants, soldiers, economic and business enterprises, children, adolescents, and the aging. Even Party newspapers are published to meet the distinctive needs of central, provincial, and county governments. This multi-layered structure is necessary if newspapers are to remain vital to their distinct readerships. Can we not also develop different newspapers according to reader educational level or according to newspaper administrative systems or the like? The question is worth serious consideration.

Newspapers might successfully address various educational levels

The Central Propaganda Department's July 1983 document on "strengthening propaganda and patriotic education" articulated an important premise: "Because the caliber of individual thought, consciousness, and educability differ, our education on philosophy and politics should be carried out at different levels, too. We should gradually implement a system whereby education on patriotism, collectivism, socialism, and communism is implemented at different levels." If, as this document also states, patriotism "has a solid foundation in public opinion and social psychology [and] can be understood and accepted by a wide range of social members of different cultural levels with different thought processes and levels of consciousness," then why do we not restructure our newspaper system to more effectively accommodate multi-layered propaganda?

Newspapers need not be identical

Even daily papers can speak to different segments of the population. The aim of our daily Party newspapers is: (1) to educate the readership toward socialist and communist thought; (2) to prioritize that content which promotes Party policy; (3) to direct the workforce; and (4) to target as their readership the advanced elements of the Party cadres and the proletariat.

Even as we preserve the integrity of these newspapers, could we not also launch other comprehensive newspapers whose aim might be to promote love of country, love of neighbor, and understanding of and obedience to the law—each targeting the common masses as their readership? Content might include interviews and reports on subjects that concern the proletariat. The proposition here is that such a plan would likely increase readership. In fact, such is already the case in major markets.

The Shanghai-based *Young Generation Magazine* targets young people. Its theme of patriotism, law, and morality has developed a loyal readership. Since its inception in 1991, its monthly subscriptions have increased by an average of 100,000 per issue, with annual subscriptions reaching almost five million by the end of 1996. When intellectual and political education is targeted at distinct audiences, readership experiences rapid, exponential growth.

A three-tiered structure

An identifying characteristic of Chinese newspapers is their accountability, not only to the Constitution and the law, but also to their respective Party organs. May we not keep this system intact and still try out one or two daily newspapers that would be responsible only to the Constitution and the law? The chief directors of these newspapers would, of course, be appointed or approved by the Party and the government, but a flexible editorial administration, thus sanctioned, would promote an innovative, creative environment, thus benefiting the reform process of the whole press industry.

A three-tiered newspaper structure launched to protect and to serve (1) the integrity of the Party, (2) the critical demands of our governing entities, and (3) the interests of the proletariat would soar as one perfect, three-staged rocket in the service of socialism and the people.

Macro-Issue 2—Introduce the Successful Format of our Foreign-Oriented News Reports into Domestic Reporting

In 1979, there was a move within the industry to improve the quality of the domestic news that Xinhua[3] sent to overseas services. For that purpose, Hu Qiaomu[4] suggested doing systematic research on Xinhua's experiences with the Voice of America and the British Broadcasting Company. He also expressed hope that the most successful formats would find their way into Xinhua's domestic service. These suggestions offer valuable guidance today for both our foreign and domestic reporting.

In recent years, there have been many changes in our reports for overseas news services. We have significantly moderated our eagerness to get the story out quickly, our impatience for instant feedback, and our overt proselytizing. Although foreign audiences are still not very satisfied with China's foreign reports, innovations have already rejuvenated our domestic news. Many Chinese readers enjoy these China News

Agency[5] and Xinhua stories because they address audience needs, they employ more subtle means of propaganda, and they have assimilated a measure of the Western reporting style.

One critical question emerges as worthy of research: why can't our domestic media use these more effective reporting styles in stories to foreign markets? There was a time when domestic newspapers occasionally published foreign-bound China News Agency reports. Because the practice proved effective, it should now be beyond reproach.

I want to make a bold suggestion: that the China News Agency could send its news in a single format to both domestic and foreign media. Each domestic media outlet could then run reports from Xinhua or the China News Agency according its own need and nature. Competition would emerge between the two news agencies, which would help to release editors from entrenched conventions and stimulate progress. The ensuing success would also improve public relations. Such reform could be achieved with a modicum of effort and would greatly benefit the whole press industry. In short—twice the result with half the labor.

Macro-Issue 3—Managing Newspapers as Enterprises

As early as 1950, people suggested that newspapers should be self-supporting and independent of government subsidy. In the current environment of economic reform, there is even more reason to reconsider this recommendation. Since 1950, the number of newspaper employees has multiplied fourfold. Rising paper prices, soaring publishing fees, and the like have put many newspapers in the red. More so now than ever, turning subsidized newspapers into self-sustaining enterprises would both reduce the financial burden on the government and provide numerous social benefits.

There is already evidence of the benefit of a balanced, self-sustaining press industry. For example, *Guangming Daily* and *Wen Hui Bao* have both established subsidiary science and technology service companies. By utilizing their existing expertise in information technology and communications, these enterprises have provided jobs for surplus employees and increased worker benefits. Subsidiary functions must not, of course, be allowed to supersede the media's primary purpose, and the greatest energies must continue to be given to running the newspaper.

Macro-Issue 4—Perfect the Administrative Mechanism

Even though the State Council has established a ministry specifically to administer our broadcasting industry, the myriad newspapers and magazines in China have no national administrative organ. Many newspaper professionals have suggested establishing a Press Administration

Ministry to deal with issues common to the various print media branches. Its role would be similar to that of the National News Administration, which existed during the first few years of the People's Republic of China.[6]

Macro-Issue 5—The Press's Dominant Function of Guidance Should Be Expanded to Include Social Practice

Western journalism theories emphasize the media's "watchdog" function of criticizing government, but devalue the media's crucial mouthpiece function.[7] Conversely, China's journalism theories have traditionally stressed only the "guiding/mouthpiece" function—the Party's and government's practice of guiding the workforce through newspapers—while hardly touching upon newspapers' supervision of government. (What limited "watchdog" function there is, is usually confined to high-level government newspapers, publicly criticizing the work being done in lower-level government offices.)

In my opinion, the foremost role of the socialist press is to guide the socialist system, communicating valuable information from the top down. But if we take a fair and sober look at the severely harmful role the press has played since the establishment of the People's Republic of China, and if we carefully and objectively examine the accomplishments and failures of the socialist press worldwide, it becomes readily apparent that journalism should also function to supervise the socialist system by communicating invaluable perspectives from the bottom up.

Certainly, development of this sort must be a gradual process and would proceed in tandem with the development of social democracy and legislation. Overnight development is impossible, but research on the guiding principles of the press industry and journalism theory should confirm that such development is necessary.

ENTHUSIASTICALLY SUPPORT AND PARTICIPATE IN PRESS REFORM

Commencing real and practical press reform will demand a fighting spirit, enthusiastic support, and active participation in the reforms themselves.

Respect the Sensitivity of the News

Be bold in reform, but reform carefully. The lackadaisical public attitude toward press reform—and the resultant inaction—stem from the fact that people are accustomed to seeing the news as inextricably linked to politics; that the press industry is part and parcel of an inviolable sector. Actually, the close link between news and politics simply serves to illustrate the special importance of press reform.

Whether or not a topic is sensitive is not the primary issue; the issue is whether it can be handled properly. In the past, meetings on foreign affairs were reported according to the TASS[8] news agency model. Reports were framed in words like, "The meeting is being held in a 'friendly,' or 'frank,' or 'friendly and frank' atmosphere." This style never remotely addressed the meeting's agenda. The outside world was left to surmise what transpired by interpreting the intensities of adjectives. What drove this was a compulsive concern for the "sensitivity" of the agenda being reported and a fear that if the report was not appropriately handled, it might easily have a negative political consequence.

We have made progress in recent years. Now we report part of a meeting's agenda and use quotes from both sides. As a result, faster distribution of information has won approval from the wider audience. Why should we not continue this practice? This illustrates a rule:

Once you move ahead and do it, a hard thing can become easy. But if you never try, an easy thing can become very hard.

Let Go of the Idea that Everything Must Be Thought Out and Researched before We Can Begin

We must stick to the principle that we will learn most by doing, and move ahead to create a press with Chinese characteristics.

At present, press reform remains suspended until more research can be done; the premise being that we do not yet have enough information. Theoretical research is important and must indeed proceed, but we cannot postpone press reform until all research is complete.

We should be encouraging every possible beneficial innovation in press practice. Then we can scientifically study each one, in turn, to enrich and develop existing theory. Some of the new ideas and new practices will be hard to explain within the framework of conventional theories, but insofar as each proves beneficial and sits well with the public, it should be permitted to develop. With full support, each innovation would then grow stronger.

The Information Age, the market economy's development, and an ever-increasing demand for more and faster information have brought about a corresponding demand for diverse newspapers. Every month sees a marked increase in licensing applications for new consulting newspapers, privately owned newspapers, economic development zone newspapers, and so on. This is as it should be. However, some do not support this trend. As the following story illustrates, the only possible reason for their objection is intractability.

Two Anhui Province journalists launched a specialized technology newspaper and hired a small staff. The paper, which bridges production and technology, has accumulated a sizable and appreciative audience. It is economically independent and annually brings in tens of thousands of yuan for the government. Even so, some onlookers have lodged complaints against the paper and even intend to frame a case against it.[9] Such destructive, unfounded criticism hurts press reform, particularly effective reform of the press's administrative mechanism.

The system we have today developed from the Party newspaper mechanism during revolutionary times. From those noble beginnings, the system should have acquired Chinese characteristics, building upon the excellent traditions of the progressive and revolutionary newspapers. Instead, in the 1950s, our university *Pravda-* and TASS-style newspapers mimicked the Soviet press. Although our early publications learned from those models, we fell under the influence of the Soviet models' dogmatism and so forfeited the chance to form a press based upon our own needs.

Now, theory and practice must define a "socialist press industry with Chinese characteristics." This is a daunting project, but press reform must emanate from this central concern.

Conduct Comprehensive Surveys and Research, Thereby Promoting Breakthroughs

We must no longer be content to be armchair strategists. Unless we use our energies to actively seek out breakthroughs, we only fight on paper. If reform is limited to format, we will revert to past practices.

More productive questions demand deep and careful investigation: What breakthrough will engender reform of the whole press industry? What breakthrough will reform individual press units?

China's economic reform has focused on major, state-owned enterprise. However, reform breakthrough came through "breaking the large-pot meal" (egalitarianism), which serendipitously developed in collectively owned enterprises and was then allowed to play itself out in state-owned businesses.

This same "breakthrough" strategy will inform our task. The focus of press reform should, of course, be our numerous official newspapers. However, reform in these newspapers is hard to promote because of entrenched habits formed over many years. Moreover, since official newspapers shoulder particular responsibilities, conditions for their reform naturally differ from those for common newspapers.

The decisive breakthroughs in press reform could come from a number of places. Some researchers think a breakthrough in overall press reform will happen as new types of newspapers are created. This makes sense.

Some foresee a breakthrough if the state reduces the number of newspaper subscriptions purchased with public money. This sounds reasonable, too.

Bold, sound thinking on this issue will be the most productive route to sound reform. Our efforts must concentrate on determining from where the breakthroughs may come. With strong support from other sectors, informed reform will substantially benefit society.

NOTES

1. The Third Plenum marked the formal end of the era of Mao Zedong and his followers and the beginning of Deng Xiaoping's consolidation of power.

2. From 1935 to 1946, Yan'an City was the base of the Communist Party and the Red Army.

3. The New China News Agency is China's central news agency.

4. Hu Qiaomu (1912–92) was a member of the Political Bureau with responsibility for the press sector.

5. The New China News Agency, launched in 1952, is a nongovernmental news agency. It was set up in 1952 by celebrated journalists from China's press circle and those returned from overseas. It typically targets overseas Chinese language media and is known for wide-ranging content and active reporting styles.

6. More than two years after this article was published, the State Press and Publication Administration was established, ending the period when news was administered by the Party's propaganda department.

7. See, for example, Vincent Blasi, "The Checking Value in First Amendment Theory," *American Bar Foundation Research Journal* 523, 1977.

8. TASS stands for Telegrafnoe Agenstvo Sovietskogo Soyuza (Telegraph Agency of the Soviet Union). TASS was the Soviet wire service.

9. The *Anhui Technology Newspaper* was eventually ordered to close.

CHAPTER 6

Renewing Our Concept of Journalism

This article was published in 1987, in the first issue of Hong Kong's *Panorama*. The same issue carried a review: "The Way Out for Mainland Press Reform: Introduction to an Eye-Catching Article by Sun Xupei."

At the time, Chinese society was experiencing the first stirrings of open reform. In the cities, students were beginning to take to the streets to demonstrate. My article, which discussed new concepts of press reform, naturally became the subject of examination.

At times, society can advance quickly. By the end of that year, this article was permitted publication on the mainland in *Journalism Journal*, although I was later reproached for it.

China is going through a period of reform in all sectors: economic, political, cultural, and societal. The press must play an important role in promoting these reforms and must itself undergo reform in the process. All significant transformations are rooted in the renewal of ideas. If the press is to open the door to its reform, it must do the work necessary to establish new concepts and shed outmoded ones. The purpose of this article is to express general, guiding concepts for the development and renewal of journalism ideas from four perspectives: (1) developing a tri-level press industry, (2) expanding the volume of information, (3) reflecting different voices, and (4) revamping propaganda concepts and reporting methods.

China's journalism has distinctive, positive attributes. The press has played a critical role in the development of socialism; its achievements must not be underestimated. However, because of limitations in space, this article will analyze those segments that need development and reform. In addition, because the article is about the renewal of ideas, it can be only an exploratory discussion. As my argument may be imperfect during my own "renewing," I sincerely solicit criticism and correction from readers.

DEVELOPING A MULTI-LEVELED SOCIALIST PRESS

To understand the need for a multi-layered press, one must first appreciate the inadvisability of the practice of promoting socialism through only one agency. The only result is a rigid, sluggish environment, whether in the economy, politics, or culture. All current reform in various societal sectors is intended to cast off this mode. The "centralized ownership" economic model has become a multi-ownership system, with state ownership as the core. Unified Party leadership has progressed to divided authority between the Party and the government, which is subsequently encouraging still further division of power and supervision.

The same should be true of our ideology. Communists regard a communist society as our highest ideal. But does this imply that only those ideas that espouse communism should be accepted and all other culture and thought should be excluded? Such a practice will absolutely never work; we have already learned that lesson. Humanity's spiritual and intellectual worlds are multi-layered, as are the different levels of thought. This objective reality must be respected.

While holding to the highest communist ideal, the Sixth Plenum of the Twelfth Party Congress (1986) called on society to aggregate the various nationalities within China, and to become a highly cultivated, democratic, socialist, and modern country.[1] With this multi-level concept as the basis, we can, as the plenum's resolution states, "overcome the narrow-minded ideas that have long caused serious damage" and unite every sector of our society, from communists to people with religious belief. The resolution declared,

All positive thoughts and spirits which are beneficial to achieving the four modernizations [agriculture, industry, science, and national defense]; *all* positive thoughts and spirits which are beneficial to unifying different peoples, advancing society, and ensuring the well-being of the people; and *all* positive thoughts and spirits which advocate earning a fine and admirable life through honest labor, should be respected, protected and developed.

These "three 'all's'" mean that all positive thoughts and spirits can be regarded as part of socialist intellectual cultivation. What an enlightened policy on thought and culture!

As an important aspect of thought and culture, the press should also be multi-layered. Developing a multi-layered, multifarious press has already become an important factor in socialist intellectual cultivation. Newspapers are published for workers, peasants, and the army; for metal workers, coal workers, and petroleum workers; for old people, children, and teenagers; and in the form of daily newspapers, evening newspapers, and morning newspapers.

Now that we may have different levels of "thought and spirit" (insofar as they are positive), and may justifiably be at different stages in the evolution of our thought, should we not also have newspapers of different styles? Should we not develop newspapers attuned to the different levels of thought?[2]

Socialist journalism originated with the Communist newspapers—as they existed before the Party secured political power. But after establishing new China, we devised a new press—the people's press—where Party and non-Party newspapers coexisted, as did state-owned, collectively owned, and privately owned newspapers. Our press system at that time had multiple levels, with newspapers of various purposes, management styles, and tone.

In the press reform that occurred after 1952, Premier Zhou Enlai and others called for retaining at least some of the collectively owned newspapers, but those calls were not heeded. For various reasons—among them, the opinion that "only unity and one voice is socialism"—the different levels of the press disappeared. No longer was there a distinction between Party and government newspapers or between state and nongovernment ownership. Abolished was the special government branch that administered the press sector. Party committees administered newspapers, and the thousands of Party newspapers were published with a uniform face and uniform opinions.

Such a mechanism has benefited the development of neither internal Party nor popular democracy. It has shackled the press to the extent that "when the Party errs, all newspapers err." And, as a result, the news media have muzzled public opinion, strangled democracy, and corroded the nation's political life.

Fortunately, since the Third Plenum of the Eleventh Party Congress in 1978, China's press has been rapidly evolving. By March 1985, China had more than 2,300 newspapers, of which 1,776 had won formal licenses. As of this writing, 1,008 more newspapers had been established. The types and functions of newspapers are more diverse than ever before, and the quality of the rejuvenated Party newspapers has improved.

Non-Party newspapers have been developing rapidly. Newspapers recently launched by the Chinese People's Political Consultative Conference, by China's democratic parties, and by overseas Chinese—all stressing love of the motherland and home—have provided the framework for diversification. More than forty new collectively owned newspapers evidence the first budding of multiple ownership in the newspaper industry. A multi-layered, socialist press model could provide a basis from which to renovate China's journalism.

SATISFY READER DEMAND FOR NEWS TO THE GREATEST EXTENT POSSIBLE

The basic mission of socialist newspapers and the fundamental goals of press reform are the same: to satisfy—in a timely fashion—reader demand for news and the public's need to learn about major domestic and foreign events. These goals seem unreachable under the current system. In that case, realizing them will mean challenging and changing convention.

Newspapers have many functions: publishing news, transmitting opinions, spreading technology, supplying entertainment, and promoting the sale of products. In China, only the function of transmitting opinions (the "mouthpiece" function) has been consistently strengthened over time, and that has been limited to communicating government propaganda from the top down, neglecting transmission of public feedback or "supervision" from the bottom up.

The outmoded concept of newspapers as "tools of class struggle" and "propaganda tools" defines newspapers by a single function typical of a single period from a single perspective. That particular function is emphasized to such a degree that it supersedes and ultimately displaces all other functions. In the end, only newspaper reports that benefit propaganda can be published.

The time we live in is totally different from revolutionary times and the "class struggle" that followed the establishment of the People's Republic of China. In the past, news media were required to act only as revolutionary "wind-blowers" or trumpets of class struggle. The first daily papers of the Chinese Communist Party were full of ardent commentary and published little, if any, news.

That was appropriate for the time, but now we are engaged in socialist modernization. Modern readers demand that their newspapers and broadcast stations exercise all their functions, especially that of spreading news and information. In an Information Age—and especially against the background of development and market economics—journalism should be a bridge between and among society's echelons.

Entrepreneurs in Shanghai care about the Jialin Group of Sichuan; university students in coastal regions care about the scenic beauty of the

Qinghai-Xizang Plateau; fishing companies in Zhoushan care about the fishing industry in Denmark and Norway; and peasants across the country care about the production and sale of agricultural products in their own provinces and abroad. This significant public concern for economic news will soon be followed by concern about political news. In fact, coverage of the recent case of Bu Xingsheng, a well-known reformer, aroused discussion among reformers across the nation.

To meet these emerging needs, newspaper editors and their staff must become increasingly well informed, and their reports must be detailed and accurate. Otherwise, they will not be able to satisfy public demand.

In general, however, the propaganda-style reports and other practices that show no respect for reader demands remain essentially unchanged. Most of our papers offer only narrow coverage. Most available space is filled with repetitive, so-called "work-directing" news (usually unrecognizable as news). As a result, informative stories have been few and far between. Stories that particularly interest readers, such as lifestyle stories, disaster pieces, and coverage of fantastic and unusual events, have been rarer still. Despite an increase in the number of stories, information content is still lacking, and readers who do pick up a paper find little to interest them.

If we are to overcome this situation, we must take propaganda value *and* news value into consideration. The value of propaganda stems from its function for Party newspapers and the socialist necessity to guide the workforce. The value of disseminating news is to inform readers; that is their expectation. Neither value can be neglected. As newspapers masterfully measure the propaganda value of the news, so should they calibrate its news value and make every effort to publish all news worth publishing.

Another issue must be raised here: the predicament of reporting on sensitive subjects that may cause readers to react from emotion and desire. In the past, the press was prohibited from reporting on sensitive issues—stories thought likely to induce negative results or reflect the darker side of life. There was concern that publishing certain stories might promote more of the same undesirable behavior or produce an improper psychological state.

Certainly, we must exercise prudence in reporting sensitive topics, but if we intend to develop a sophisticated socialist democracy, we will have to respect the public's right to know, and upgrade political transparency. The number of reports on the government's policy-making process should increase. Although policy making is sensitive, we cannot confine coverage to policy implementation. Reporting on policy making would enable the proletariat to carry out its proper supervisory function based on a policy's objective characteristics and public impact.

As a general rule, newspapers are obliged to supply the public with timely reports on the nation's political and social life. We must reduce limitations on stories feared to evoke negative reader response. We must emphasize the service that literature, the arts, and all mass communications share: the manifestation and reflection of human emotion.

Newspapers that accurately and responsibly reflect the proletariat's voice and serve as true and effective outlets for their feelings on contemporary issues will not only reinforce readers' relationship with newspapers, but also enhance the psychological stability, perspective, and unity of the society they serve.

Disaster and accident coverage and feature stories should also be reevaluated in line with the development of the market economy. A single news report about damage to a disaster-stricken area might provide decision-making information to both the factories that depend on raw material from that area and enterprises that might meet that area's needs. A feature story covered a swindler who told strangers he had access to sought-after TV sets and then stole their money. Another reported on a group of peasants who were stopping trucks to rob them of fertilizer. Such information makes the populace aware of difficult social conditions, even as it informs businesses and government policy makers who must be aware of such matters. Journalism will work better for the people if it operates under a more functional system.

DIFFERENTIATE AMONG THE VARIOUS FORMS OF OPINION IN OUR SOCIETY, AND DEVELOP SUPERVISION BY PUBLIC OPINION

Another important newspaper function is the distribution of information. Through this mechanism come propaganda, guidance, criticism, and supervision. Party newspapers communicate Party policies and thereby guide work, a tradition that should be venerated and developed. But we have yet to move journalism beyond these functions to become a facilitating channel through which the upper echelons guide the lower and through which credible information from the proletariat guides the upper echelons.

In a centralized system, the news media operate solely as the propaganda tools of the people in power and the government. As such, they must praise the message they proclaim. They may not carry opposing viewpoints. Policy analysis, suggestions, and criticism are relegated to the limited system of face-to-face communications, speeches at meetings, or letters to successively higher levels of government.

Although some information makes it through this person-to-person communication system, most of the information the leadership ultimately receives has been adjusted for the hearer's benefit, such that messages usually take the form, "I support what you support, only more so!

I oppose what you oppose, but with twice the fervor!" Compounded by the dearth of opposing views in the media, the result is a severely unreliable information structure, harmful to both policy implementation and the decision-making process itself.

Developing Opinion Markets

To carry out effective reform, we must develop a workable model for responsible criticism and policy supervision. The media can make good use of valuable, forthright input by establishing a "market of opinions," that is, publication of all opinions that do not run counter to the Constitution and laws, including praise, affirmation, criticism, and supervision.

Everyone acknowledges that we have various kinds of markets. Can we not also have an "opinion market"? The answer will emerge only after careful consideration.

For the thousands of years of China's feudal society, speech and literature were subjected to bans and inquisitions. Certainly there was no "opinion market." Even though feudal courts positioned such forms of person-to-person communication as argument and/or tolerable remonstration, protesters were frequently put to death. This gave rise to the saying "Civil officials die in protest; military officers die in battle." Even though some feudal rulers were "wise kings" and "upright officials who wear the clothing of the common man to conduct investigations," all of them enforced an absolute ban on writing books or establishing newspapers to express political opinion.

Socialist politics is the people's politics—open politics which, in turn, depend upon freedom of speech and publication. Therefore, establishing open opinion markets is natural and reasonable.

In his *October Revolution*, Lenin said, "Freedom of publication means that all citizens can express all their opinions freely."[3] An opinion market administered according to law is crucial to socialist construction. It enables decision makers and directors to know the range of the people's will in the shortest time possible and so to select sound strategies for the country's stability and prosperity.

To encourage the expression of public opinion and establish opinion markets, our newspapers—including Party newspapers—should reflect the full spectrum of the public voice. Thus, newspaper content would manifest a harmonious, multi-layered structure that speaks with both informed authority and representative opinion.

Such a proposal is in full accord with the consistent stance of our Party. In 1956, the Central Committee of the Chinese Communist Party wrote the following in response to a letter from the editorial staff of *The People's Daily*.[4]

In order to facilitate the publication of discussions on various opinions in news-papers, *The People's Daily* should stress that it is both the central government's official newspaper and the people's newspaper. In the past, there was an opinion that "every word of *The People's Daily* should represent opinions of the central government," and "all comments published in the newspaper should be com-pletely correct, including readers' letters."

Of course, in the newspapers of 1956, these principles were impossible to put into practice and would have compromised the Party's political image. However, in the present climate, all the articles in *The People's Daily* need not represent opinions of the central government. A portion of the articles and editorials should come from government and Party leaders. In addition, some writers should be permitted to publish views that may be contrary to the Party. This can help activate thoughts and help Marxist truth become increasingly clear through de-bate.

These instructions are vital to socialist journalism! And yet, for more than three decades, interruptions of Leftist thought have made it impos-sible to implement them.

Creating the Model

We must create a workable model by educating readers as to the var-ious types and "levels" of newspaper comments. As they learn about editorials, authoritative platforms, commentators' articles (with and without bylines), short comments, editors' notes, and readers' forums, they would gain a clear understanding of each of the different functions. Readers must be helped to understand which of these carry the opinions of the central government, which carry journalists' opinions, and which are the views of readers of different classes.

When Marx was the chief editor of *Rheinische Zeitung*, he set a hori-zontal line across the middle of the newspaper. Above the line were opinion articles by the editorial department. Below the line were opinion articles submitted by the public. Each respective author was responsible for the content.

Might we not create a column called "Readers' Forum," accompanied by a short sentence such as, "Please select the worthwhile opinions from the following"? The readers would then understand that the column was simply a collection of different opinions that should be taken only as points of reference. A Readers' Forum like this would promote discus-sion of sensitive issues that have thus far been avoided. Hearsay and secret talk would be transformed to open discussion guided by news-papers. We would truly overcome the criticism so frequently voiced by the public: "The things I care about are not discussed; the things about which I care nothing, you write of again and again."

The entrenched notion that "promoting public opinion supervision will cause thought chaos and make it hard to promote policy" is ground-less. There may have been foundation for it when law had no power and newspapers and editorials were used to rule the country. But when a legal system is complete and a country is being ruled according to law, newspapers simply exercise a form of psychological power (in social science terms, "flexible social control"). Law and political order hold the definitive, binding power (or "firm social control").

To date, public opinion has kept up with the development and imple-mentation of law. Moreover, if the news media's coordinated functions are scientifically and reasonably introduced—particularly the social func-tion of public opinion supervision—the public's social-psychological en-durance will be incrementally strengthened. They will be able to discern the "main melody" from the rich "symphony" of thought that accom-panies it.

Even the most extreme commentary is not worth worrying about. The well-known modern journalist Liang Qichao said eighty years ago,

[Even if a newspaper article] appears to be radical, that should not be considered a shortcoming. Why? Because, while I am radical in one extreme, there will be someone radical to the opposite extreme to balance my opinions and someone who will tend to intermediate to fashion a compromise between the two. Opin-ions depend upon each other; they debate with each other; they compromise with each other. The truth must then emerge. . . . [5]

RENEWING OUR IDEAS ABOUT JOURNALISM AND REPORTING

Our traditional journalism has depended upon content propagated from above. Propaganda departments disseminated stories about Party spirit, class characteristics, appropriate ideological levels, a fighting spirit, and social guidance. Even though we affect concern for readership, audience research has never been a priority. As a result, all newspapers look alike—newspaper directors perpetuate the pattern, whether or not it works, and readers must endure it, whether or not they like it.

This situation must change immediately. Extensive scientific research has been done on the effect of modern mass communications on the audience, and we should take that research to heart. We must acquire a thorough understanding of the psychology of modern information con-sumers and carefully explore the psychology of propaganda. Then, using that information, we must abolish outmoded ideas and replace outdated propaganda strategies.

Revolutionary propaganda is appropriate for revolutions. Lenin ad-vocated "instilling," saturating workers in Marxism. If propaganda is also essential to present-day and future China, it must be with the understanding that different historic periods require distinctive messages, targets, and propaganda strategies.

When China's revolutionary and counterrevolutionary forces struggled with each other, we employed "shouting" agitation, "saturation" propaganda, and published leaflet-style papers that carried significantly more political agitation than news. Newspapers had to do more than advocate socialism and a sense of the Party; they needed to bolster a fighting spirit.

Today's political atmosphere is much different. The establishment of sovereign, proletariat political power must shape every facet of propaganda, from its mission to the means by which it most appropriately influences the public it serves. The associated rise in cultural and educational levels and the development of political and social democracy have occasioned proletarian readers to demand more extensive, objective, and varied coverage. They require newspapers to function as peers who respect their judgment. The adage "The stronger the propaganda tone and dazzling the fighting spirit, the bigger the readership" is already outdated.

Disdain for naked propaganda is now worldwide. In Western countries, "propaganda" is a derogatory term. Such is the case in the East as well. Certain scholars believe that aversion to the term began with the charged rhetoric between the West and the East after World War II. During those years, the propaganda on the Voice of America (VOA) soon took the form of anti-communist diatribes. Eventually, the ineffectiveness of that kind of propaganda was realized, as a number of VOA station directors resigned in protest. Finally, in the 1970s, VOA changed its "propaganda" delivery style, adopting a format of accurate, objective, and wider coverage, factual and balanced news, and a clear distinction between news and commentary. The dramatic changes not only preserved the broadcasts' effectiveness as propaganda, but actually enhanced the station's image as a genuine "voice of America."

The substantive differences between Eastern and Western propaganda must not preclude comparative research. Both are propaganda, and as such, share common precepts. Effective reform of our propaganda system demands that we follow these common precepts. We must reject the notion that "propaganda must affect instant change and the desired results" and replace it with a view of propaganda as a subtle, imperceptible influence. We must alter our practice of limiting its objective to "instilling" and develop an attitude of respect toward readers' judgment.

MAKING A PRIORITY OF OBJECTIVE REPORTING AND FAIR COMMENTARY

In 1956, Liu Shaoqi, then Party vice chairman, pointed out that news stories should be authentic, balanced, objective, and fair.[6] This is a central tenet of news coverage, but we have been afraid of it for years. In fact, objective, fair articles have been typically criticized as "capitalist journalism thought." Whenever the issues of objectivity and fairness were raised, someone would attach the word "absolute" and then launch into criticism on that basis.

Journalism practice has already proved that a news story can integrate point of view, objectivity, and fairness. We must put our best efforts toward moving even further in this direction and gradually diminish the quantity and intensity of propaganda in our newspapers. As we persist in our efforts, we will see greater and greater rewards. We must begin with two projects.

We Must Move Past Our Customary Practice of Using Propaganda to Effect Total and Immediate Transformation of the Masses

This all-or-nothing lunge at creating public opinion has been used for many years, but it no longer serves the political interests of our society. The saying is common among the people: "The louder the propaganda, the worse it is likely to be for the country!"

The wise decision to carry out gradual urban economic reform provides a clear example. As urban economic reform was about to be made public through the media, central government leaders insisted that it be released in small increments. They thought the people—who may or may not have understood the rationale—might blindly rush toward abrupt change. With measured implementation, a chaotic "rush to reform" could be averted.

Rather than "gathering in haste and dispersing in turmoil," newspaper propaganda should convey influence without being noticed. It should "wet the plants without making any sound." This practice may at first seem too slow, but it corresponds to the pace of the natural development of things.

Outmoded News Writing Strategies Should Also Be Changed

Our current system operates under the notion that all propaganda efforts—no matter how limited their focus—should be targeted to the masses, and thereby, effect nationwide transformation.

For example, the public is repeatedly assured that the appointment of one person will save an entire factory, or that implementation of a new wage policy will single-handedly cause the export trade to boom. These "single-cause" strategies mold "news" to the prevailing political situation. This neither reflects modern life nor accommodates modern readers.

The public knows that multiple reasons exist for any given reform. Over-simplification merely serves to reduce newspaper credibility.

Propaganda writing must also follow tightly prescribed standards. For example, positive reports may carry no criticism, and critical reports may not include affirmation. That kind of reporting is unrealistic—absolutely good or absolutely bad things do not exist in the world. Reports that promote a given change should also point out its possible limitations. Conversely, critical reports should also include that recommendation's potential or realized gains.

Effective propaganda reform must replace blanket media campaigns that promote instantaneous change with objective reports and balanced commentary.

NOTES

1. The "Resolution on the Guiding Principles for Construction of Socialist Spiritual Civilization" was adopted on September 28, 1986.

2. The Propaganda Ministry once proposed four levels of thinking: communism, socialism, group spirit, and patriotism, respectively.

3. First articulated by Lenin during the October Revolution. First published in "How to Guarantee the Success of a Press Law in the Constitutional Conference," *Workers' Road*, September 15(28), 1917. (September 15 is the date on the Russian calendar.)

4. The original phrasing of this offers an insight into China's bureaucracy and into the process of informing policy by writing "letters." A literal translation of this passage reads, "The Central Committee of the Chinese Communist Party responded to a letter written as the result of a meeting of the editors of *The People's Daily* and sent to the Communist Party." It is important to Sun's argument to (a) show that the letter had proceeded through proper channels, (b) show the source of the original concern, and (c) justify the stature of those involved.

5. "Words to Colleagues with Respect" (1906), in *The Complete Works of Cold Drink Room (Middle)*, Liang Qichao, China Publishing House, 1948.

6. Speech to Xinhua News Agency (1956).

CHAPTER 7

Effective Press Reform within a Socialist Market Economy

Since 1984, I have published several articles proposing recommendations for broad-based, systematic press reform. Most of my energy the first five years was spent articulating, disseminating, and defending those proposals. Although the articles engendered a measure of academic discussion, their primary effect was to cause me trouble. It seemed that I was fighting in isolation. I was ready to give up a losing battle.

But when, in 1992, the Party accepted Deng Xiaoping's socialist market economic theories, I realized that the time had come for me to declare war on prevailing concepts such as, "To implement the planned economy, we must implement 'planned news.' "

By January 1993, this article was complete. Some of my colleagues said it challenged existing press policy on many points. In 1994, it and a series of my articles on press freedom, legislation, and reform were compiled into a book titled *New Journalism Theories*. After its publication, I was considered no longer suitable to remain as director of the Institute of Journalism in the Chinese Academy of Social Sciences.

THE RELATIONSHIP BETWEEN THE JOURNALISM INDUSTRY AND THE ECONOMY

In May and June of 1956, Mao Zedong said: "In socialist countries, newspapers reflect the socialist economy. A planned economy based on public ownership is accomplished when the news serves as an economic tool. . . . In contrast," he said, "as economic tools of capitalism, capitalist newspapers trigger an uncontrolled economy and promote competition among groups of citizens."[1] Mao also criticized some of the new, intellectual communists as being "against necessary and appropriate centralized leadership and against the planning and controlling of culture and education [including the news industry] necessary to achieving a planned economy."[2] Edicts such as this one have formed the theoretical basis of our journalism for decades.

Mao is correct to argue that, because a socialist journalism industry is rooted in a socialist economy, the industry should serve that economy. The Constitution itself provides that the news/broadcasting industry "serves the people *and* serves socialism."

What needs delineation is the difference between the meta-function of ultimate service to socialism and categorically deciding the exact forms of service to be supplied and the way the industry should function. These are two different things. We cannot simplistically equate news that serves a free economy with the capitalist press, or news that serves a planned economy with the socialist press.

Notwithstanding their alignment to disparate social structures, the socialist press and capitalist press have many common operating principles. For example, all news media exist to convey information and opinion—including *thoughts*: the expression of broad perspectives; *viewpoints*: the expression of more specific perspectives; and *plans*: the most focused form of expression. Both socialist and capitalist constitutions provide that citizens have freedom of speech and publication, which are then manifested through freedom of the press. Press freedom, regulated by law and journalistic ethics, is essential in any society for the purpose of relating the changing circumstances and the differing viewpoints that characterize the society. These principles should be self-evident.

However, in China, the underlying guideline of journalism for decades has been, "A planned newspaper is the reflection of planned economy." Mao's goals for a "necessary and appropriately centralized leadership" and the "planning and controlling of journalism" have not been realized.

In fact, as Deng Xiaoping pointed out with penetrating insight, "We long believed that a socialist, planned-administration system must use a highly centralized administration mechanism on economy, politics, culture and society."[3] We had achieved a highly centralized, "planned news." But that news media functioned only as a tool of propaganda, operating according to the dictates of the administrative organs.

Since the founding of the People's Republic of China (PRC), so-called "unified expression in propaganda" has governed what journalists report and how they report it. Reporters for both departmental and national/ regional papers are expected to wage "propaganda battles by writing according to monthly propaganda outlines."

An important feature of "planned news" has been that all of the news media have uniformly reported a prescribed viewpoint. The dominion of "news, old news, and non-news" has been part and parcel of the system. "Old news" refers to the intentional neglect of timeliness, deliberately suppressing news until it becomes stale. (When Lin Biao[4] died in an airplane crash in Mongolia, the story was released several weeks after the event. The death toll of the Tangshan earthquake was withheld until many years afterward.) "Non-news" means a story will not be reported, no matter what its importance to common citizens (as when China's public media reported nothing when humans landed on the moon).

This point by no means negates the legitimacy of news selection, of differentiation between primary and secondary news, or of various reporting angles. Any medium must select and handle news according to its own editing principles. Furthermore, it may be wise to give no coverage to stories that compromise national security or individual privacy.

But when news that has nothing to do with national security or individual privacy is suppressed and turned into "old news" or "non-news," then the masses are deceived, and democratic policies are undermined. Such media cannot win the public trust, nor can they hope to play a constructive role in the nation's political and social life. On the contrary, that influence is negative and even destructive. The examples have been too many to list here.

The press reform that has been in process since the 1978 Third Plenary Session of the eleventh Party Central Committee[5] would have drastically changed the appearance and, to a large extent, the substance of China's news media. However, because of the intransigence of the "planned newspaper is the reflection of planned economy" theory, it has remained difficult to recommend and implement the reforms.

Fortunately, a new impetus for press reform has emerged. In 1992, the Party's fourteenth National Congress noted that effective development of the socialist market economy necessitates promotion of related reform in the cultural sector. If "planned news" was counterproductive even under a planned economy, it will be even more detrimental to a market economy. It then follows that if a planned economy would have benefitted from a degree of freedom and accountability to law, a market economy will benefit even more.

In China's highly centralized, planned economy, the news media belonged to the propaganda sector and were accordingly relegated to the status of elements in society's political superstructure.[6] That was their role in class and political struggles. Under current market-economy conditions, the press serves as superstructure *and* as foundation. As propaganda's mouthpiece, it continues to serve the political purposes of the ruling party by articulating government guidelines, policies, and viewpoints. But as an information *industry* within the market economy, the press is foundational as well. News and information serve as a type of "third" (social service) industry product,[7] and as such, function as a consumer commodity.

Formerly, the news media's locus was politics. Today, that locus must be economics. In the process of developing the market economy, we should research and develop our journalism industry primarily as an information industry to carry out informed production, circulation, and consumption of information. This demands historic change.

SIGNIFICANTLY INCREASE THE AMOUNT OF INFORMATION AVAILABLE

Over the past few hundred years, the global journalism industry has developed in tandem with the rise of market economies. Typically, as the division of labor in society has become increasingly elaborate, and communication has become increasingly pervasive, then society, in turn, has required progressively more information to function. In the fierce competition of a market economy, the more fully one grasps information and the more complete, accurate, and timely that information is, the more informed one's decision making will be and the more likely one is to succeed.

During the proposal of a "The Big Chinese Economic Circle,"[8] which included the PRC, Hong Kong, and Taiwan, any discussion of comparative strengths noted Hong Kong's preeminence in information and finance. In the tiny area of Hong Kong are more than sixty different newspapers, each with dozens of pages. The information supplied there by the news media alone is as vast as the open sea, not to mention the copious information supplied through other channels.

The hallmark of a society's advancement is the continuous growth of information. The more developed a market economy, the more advanced its information industry. For example, Japan boasts the largest number of newspapers per thousand people in the world. The volume of print information in Japan increased more than 200 percent from 1979 to 1989. The information volume of their electronic media in that same time period increased thirty fold. Although the volume of information provided by China's news media has historically been small, in recent years, market demand and increased advertising have encouraged the inception of

one newspaper after another. Still others have expanded. Newspapers—
including *Tianjin Daily, Jiefang Daily, Wen Hui Daily, Beijing Daily, Fujian
Daily, Heilongjiang Daily, Economics Daily*, and *Guangmin Daily*—have
doubled in size from four pages to eight. *Guangzhou Daily* has become
China's first folio, twelve-page daily newspaper, and *Xinmin Evening
Newspaper* has become China's first quarto, sixteen-page newspaper.
Meanwhile, about two-thirds of China's provincial-or city-government
newspapers and about one-third of central ministry newspapers have
added weekend editions or weekly supplements. However, since the prevailing trend of newspapers has been toward "magazinization," increase
in information volume remains limited.

Effective development of a market economy in China requires a substantial increase in the communication of information. Only when people
have access to and adequate understanding of a variety of local and
international information can they make informed decisions, adjust and
coordinate their actions in a timely fashion, and achieve a reasonable
distribution of social resources.

A recent trend provides an example. This country is in the process of
incrementally promoting a stock share-holding system. The subsequent
increase in shareholders will, in turn, increase the demand for information. Surely, a person holding shares in a number of entities cares a great
deal about economic and social development issues. The stockholder in
a textiles plant will be vitally concerned with any number of issues: the
harvest of certain cotton-production areas, a chemical fiber plant's start-
up operation, a fire in a textile plant, and/or a foreign country's import
limitation on Chinese-produced textiles. Since he can buy stocks in other
sectors at any time, he must pay attention to those other sectors and
compare their situations.

What is more, stockholder concern will cover not only economic news
but also political news. Deng Xiaoping's speeches in his Southern tour
caused the Hong Kong stock market to soar.[9] One day in June last year
[1992], the Shenzhen stock market jumped fifteen points at the mere ru-
mor that Chen Yun—a standing member of the Political Bureau and one
of China's pioneer revolutionists—was planning an investigatory trip to
Shenzhen.

People are realizing that good use of political news can also turn a
profit. According to a recent national newspaper article, one Jiangzu
Province entrepreneur has profited handsomely. The day's news indi-
cated the imminence of diplomatic ties between China and South Korea.
The same day's television news reported that during their recent visit to
Beijing, South Korean leaders were given preferential treatment. The entrepreneur then realized that Yantai in Shangdong Province, separated
from South Korea by only a small body of water, would become a hot
spot for future Korean investment, he went immediately to that city and

bought a large piece of land. Several months later, as he had expected, that city's real estate prices soared, and his enterprises profited. In market economy conditions, the public demand for a high volume of information should provide a strong stimulus for media reform.

In a market economy, it is not enough to supply information to the public from only one perspective. Different regions, different departments, and enterprises with different ownership all have different interests and demands. The one piece of information that means little to A might be crucial to B. Social demands can be satisfied only with a volume of information that sufficiently reflects that society's diversity. This is one of the reasons that newspapers in developed countries typically have several dozen and sometimes more than 100 pages per issue. Increased information volume will demand and, finally, bring about greater press freedom.

Before information volume can be increased, however, we must ascertain the answers to key research questions. How should information volume be defined? How is information volume calculated? What is the current information volume? What kinds of information need to increase significantly? How should information volume be expanded? What experience from developed countries can be referenced?

DELIBERATELY DEVELOP PUBLIC OPINION
SUPERVISION

A market economy promotes rapid development of the workforce. However, because of the diversity inherent in that workforce's economic behaviors and interests, it also has a complicated economic structure. Without appropriate restrictions, corrupt practices—such as embezzlement, bribery, and favoritism—could significantly increase. Commensurate measures are therefore essential.

Democratic systems for supervision and restriction were gradually established as each of the developed countries built its own market economy. Admittedly, these systems serve the interests of capitalists, but they also have many worthwhile aspects that can be regarded as cultural achievements and, as such, are worth our reference during the construction of our socialist market economy.

Democratic systems of supervision and restriction are important and effective remedies for corruption and provide a necessary guarantee for the healthy operation of a socialist market economy. Supervision by public opinion is among the best of those remedies.

Supervision by public opinion, communicated through the news media, is a function of press freedom. As we are developing our socialist democracy, we must also be developing a seamless mechanism for supervision by public opinion. The process will be a long one, certainly, but the first step—allowing the news media to independently expose corruption, embezzlement, and favoritism—should be put into practice as soon as possible.

"Allowing the media to independently expose corruption" means permitting the news media to make their own decisions about exposing corruption, without interference from outside elements. Correspondingly, the media must also be held fully responsible for their own reports. For example, a newspaper that slandered an individual with false or exaggerated reports would be held liable to punishment by law. This is what we mean when we say, "Reporters are responsible to the facts; newspapers are responsible to the law."

Why is it necessary for news media to be independent in exposing corruption? Because those who engage in corrupt behavior are often connected with each other and form a "relationship web" that is hard to break through. When corrupt connections are exposed through the current system, they are often quickly covered up, making investigation and disposition extremely difficult. Supervision by public opinion by its very nature can help solve this problem.

Supervision by Public Opinion Is Timely

Reporters are professional investigators and researchers, so it is easy for them to recognize clues and the "cloven hoof." The news media can publicize the "cloven hoof" promptly and objectively, and then pursue the story until the whole truth is discovered. In developed countries, many embezzlement cases have been uncovered by a reporter's vigorous investigation of some irregularity. If the media had to wait for a series of authorizations from different bureaucratic levels before they could report those initial irregularities, the wrongdoers would have that time to cover up and protect themselves, and effective public opinion supervision would be impossible.

Public Opinion Supervision Has the Benefit of Openness

Often, the initial revelation of illegal activity is just "the tip of the iceberg," but that initial report can arouse the attention of the whole society. Those who have information may be encouraged to reveal evidence to the news media and state legal entity. The resultant prompt public and government attention will make it difficult to cover up illegal activity.

Allowing the news media to independently expose corruption and other illegal activity will require a liberation of minds and a change in thinking. There has long been concern that if we expose too much corruption, it will give the public the impression that society is completely in the dark, which could affect stability and unity. Such worries are groundless. The largest current public complaint about newspapers is the plethora of favorable stories and the deficiency of those that expose corruption and illegal activity. It is obvious to everyone that corruption exists at every level of society; people will not believe that corruption is low just because the media reports so little about it. To the contrary, seeing newspapers and judicial organs expose and punish corruption will engender more confidence, both in the government and in the future. Of course, there will be initial discomfort with the change, and it will take some getting used to, but eventually everyone will realize that it is the news media's obligation to expose corruption and purify the society. The government and news media should repeatedly reinforce this point.

If we continue superficial coverage of corruption, and if we continue to insist that public opinion remain silent, then we are presenting a false picture of peace and prosperity merely to achieve a measure of temporary "social stability." But by doing this very thing, we will, in fact, be undermining our own effort against corruption and illegal activity, and in the end, social instability will be more acute than ever.

Of course, the news media cannot expose corruption simply to create a stir. They must consider the social impact of any disclosure, use scientific methods in gathering evidence, emphasize the constructive elements of criticism, and publish timely follow-up stories on how the case is being handled and any positive outcomes that result. These are the distinguishing features of socialist journalism.

DEVELOPMENT OF, AND CHANGES IN, THE
NEWSPAPER INDUSTRY

There are now more than 1,700 different newspapers in China. Most are official newspapers of party committees, government departments, and other organizations, and focus mainly on promoting the work of their sponsoring organizations. A number of cultural and entertainment newspapers have the highest concentration of technology and popular interest news. Generally speaking, however, China has no high-information-content newspapers.

Several prominent Japanese newspapers such as *Asahi Shimbun*, have 36-page morning editions and 24-page evening editions, a total of 60 pages daily. In the early 1980s, American morning and evening daily newspapers each averaged 57 and 50 pages respectively. Nothing like that has emerged in China. I am not implying that we should immediately launch 50-or 60-page newspapers, but I do think the volume of information in the Chinese news media is insufficient to meet the demands of the market economy. To increase the volume of information, we must squarely face the shortcomings of our press industry's structure: (1) confining administrative boundaries, (2) oversubsidization by the government, and (3) inappropriate distribution of space.

Chinese Newspapers Are Too Limited by Administrative Boundaries

In China, each newspaper's content has historically been limited to the local area it serves, and the entrenched practice has become the rule. Moreover, no national, comprehensive newspaper is published outside the capital, Beijing. However, to develop a market economy, the country must be able to organize production, distribution, and consumption of products in various regions, even overseas. Because production, distribution, and consumption of information must cross regions, regional and administrative isolation must end.

This does not preclude local authorities or government branches from having their own newspapers. It means that no matter where or by whom a newspaper is published, it should participate in the competition in the newspaper market with as much useful information as possible. The good ones should survive, and the inferior ones should die out.

The Issue of Government Subsidy

Popular public sentiment has it that, "The government subsidizes newspapers; the government pays subscription fees; newspapers do not worry about survival; [whether] they perform well or badly, it is the business of the government." The government can no longer afford this. There are more newspapers by the day. But as it stands, a newspaper that performs well and makes money keeps the profit. If a newspaper performs badly and loses money, it is still subsidized by the government, because that newspaper is a government propaganda tool. In some departmental newspapers, dozens to upward of 100 employees support a distribution of only 10,000–20,000 actual subscribers. Limited distribution means government subsidy, so the more such newspapers there are, the heavier the government's burden. As government moves toward structural reform, departments will become hard pressed to supply resources to such newspapers.

Newspapers Are Many; Pages Are Few; Information Volume Is Small (and Repetitive); and Advertising Space Is Limited

In the first place, this situation has created disincentives for private subscriptions. Individual readers and work units are required to take many newspapers to satisfy their information needs. This encourages government distribution over private purchase. Secondly, because the demand for advertising space is so high and the number of newspapers with national distribution is small, the advertising fees in national news- papers remain prohibitive for many potential clients. Some newspapers charge as much as 150,000 to 200,000 yuan per page (U.S. $20,000 to $25,000).

Based on this analysis, China needs to develop newspapers with the following features.

High information volume

Comprehensive newspapers with sixteen to twenty pages must be launched within the next two to three years. Such newspapers should carry both domestic and foreign news as well as technology and enter- tainment stories, and the contents should be suitable for the entire family.

Commercial characteristics

These newspapers would not need government subsidies for opera- tions or distribution, but would depend completely on the market for survival. Those newspapers that survive the competition would remain; those that fail would close down.

Popular news values

The lead story need not be limited to news about guiding work. For example, important international, social, or disaster news could all be used as the lead story on page one.

Ownership

These newspapers could be state owned, privately owned, or a hybrid of the two.

Parallel changes in the structure of all mass media would soon follow, as commercial radio stations and commercial television stations become responsible for their own profits and losses.

REFORMING NEWS CONTENT TO INFORM THE MARKET ECONOMY

In a market economy, news media coverage will need to manifest greater breadth, timeliness, and depth than it displayed under the planned economy. These improvements should ultimately apply to all forms of newspaper content; however, this discussion will focus on cov- erage of economic news.

When China operated under a planned economy, one of the key tasks of news propaganda was to promote the realization of production plans.

Reports focused on production sectors. Newspapers were used to publish stories about exemplary towns or plants. Agricultural reports discussed spring plowing, summer floods, autumn harvest, and winter reserves. Industrial reports always discussed the quality of work, touted efforts to increase productivity and save materials, and spotlighted successes. These reports had little news value and garnered no reader interest.

In a market economy, the focus of economic news reporting should be different. In the future, economic news reports should emphasize guidance *and* service.[10] The economic media will need a variety of scenarios to guide different work if that guidance is to be effective, and the service function of economic news will need to provide all of those workers with information, analysis, and forecast. Coverage that serves economic development must thus recreate its focus to provide a diverse readership with an assortment of inspirations to accommodate their own plans and activities. Perhaps this could also be considered guidance. If so, it is accomplished as the newspaper provides information service to its readers. The guidance function of newspapers is thus contained within their service function.

It may also be worth distinguishing between *propaganda about* business enterprises and *advertisements for* business enterprises. China's news media has long devoted considerable space to reporting on individual enterprises: how an enterprise develops successfully each year, how it improves its management, how it increases production and profit, how it motivates its employees, and how it values technological reform. That type of coverage may be of reference value to managers and other decision makers, or suitable for publications that primarily target entrepreneurs and government officials. But these stories have relatively little news value to the common reader, and the general populace dislikes them when they appear in general circulation newspapers. Since these articles usually occupy considerable space, readers can easily find the name of the enterprise at a glance. Thus, the primary effect of such reports is a form of advertising.

In developed countries, readers demand—and the media provide—many reports about new products created by companies or stories that feature certain entrepreneurs and their road to success. But reports written in a flattering, self-serving way about how an enterprise does its work well—like those that often appear in Chinese media—rarely appear in Western media. Such practices are considered merely another form of advertising that should be published as advertising and should identify the enterprise that paid for it. That is the rule in foreign countries.

Now China has such a rule as well. In the highly centralized, planned economy, newspapers carried no advertisements at all. Enterprises would never have considered advertising, nor would promotional articles have been construed as such. But things are different today. All enterprises have a strong sense of advertising, and all understand the close relationship between reputation and profit.

Unfortunately, they have also quickly understood that it is cheaper to "pay" a few thousand yuan to "plant" a promotional article in a newspaper than to pay the 100,000-plus yuan in advertising fees. "Payments" can take the form of money or other benefits to the newspaper, its editor, or a reporter. Despite repeated efforts to ban this widespread practice, the phenomenon persists . . . to the detriment of the professional ethical standards of journalism.

We know now that profiles of individual enterprises lack news value and cannot attract the public, that it is difficult to separate propaganda for enterprises from advertising, and that such propaganda may result in the compromise of a journalism career. If, in a market economy, the marketplace should determine the focus of economic news reports, then we need to ask a question: Can we gradually phase out reports on individual enterprises, or—if the practice must continue to some degree—report on only those businesses innovations that are worthy of being named "secret of success" stories or on new products that have public appeal?

TAKE PART IN TIMELY NEWS EXCHANGE AND COMPETITION AT HOME AND ABROAD

China's export volume already makes up nearly 20 percent of China's GNP. This means that one-fifth of the domestic economy is connected to international markets. As China's market economy develops, it will become increasingly linked to overseas markets. That trend will become obvious, especially after China joins the General Agreement on Tariffs and Trade (GATT),[11] when the Chinese economy will integrate into the world economy and compete and cooperate there. Then our communication of information will have to be far reaching, rapid, and seamless. This presents the news media with a new task: how to disseminate a large volume of information to society in a timely fashion.

Because China's news media have long been regarded as a mouthpiece and propaganda tool, both political and class orthodoxy have been stressed at the expense of the international exchange of news. That limited import and export of news is now inconsistent with China's important position in the world.

A market economy will still require the news media to retain a measure of its political and class characteristics. The news media must continue to serve socialism, should play a constructive role in promoting socialist attitudes and the Chinese people's culture, and should prevent decadent capitalist ideas from expanding their influences as news is exchanged. But the news media also belong to an information industry, and as such, that industry provides information services to the economy and society.

We should take bolder steps in the area of overseas news exchange. Practice has proved, and will continue to prove, that if we do not open our door to foreign information—if we do not have enough information about economics, politics, and culture—our managers and decision makers will be constrained to act more slowly than their foreign counterparts, and so remain at a competitive disadvantage.

In the last ten years of reform and opening, China's press has given the people a taste of less inhibited and more dynamic news and opinion. In that time, many Chinese have traveled abroad to do business, to work in plants, or to study, and they have been influenced by foreign news and information environments. All of these are conducive to consumer acceptance of still higher levels of press freedom and to no ill effect.

With the return of Hong Kong and the development of trade across the Taiwan Straits, news exchange among the mainland, Hong Kong, and Taiwan will unquestionably intensify. The agenda for that progress should include the exchange of news reports and news reporters, cooperative management and distribution of economic newspapers—even the exchange of comprehensive daily newspapers.

Information flow is essential to national unity. To promote information flow, we should progressively ease restrictions on news selection, decrease coverage of speeches, and raise the level of press freedom. In that way, government departments and officials could gradually accustom themselves to working under free-press conditions. In the same way, the people would become accustomed to choosing for themselves what is good, and adjust their own behavior accordingly.

In truth, it may be impossible to hold back increases in press freedom while we adapt to the market economy or to continue to block overseas news because we are concerned about its possible influence. For example, can China avoid developing satellite broadcasting? Certainly not.

Communication technology is both an achievement of human development and a stimulus for further development. Two important communication technologies invented by the ancient Chinese, printing and paper, have played crucial roles in propelling world progress. Microwave radios, photocopiers, international direct dial telephones, and satellite televisions all represent modern communication technologies. They too have great significance for life and productivity.

The proletariat should act to promote the development and use of communication technology to benefit the people. Resisting such technology can only put China far behind global trends and make the motherland a laughingstock. It would be as ridiculous as if we had tried to prevent Europeans from using printing and paper production technologies.

Certain Eastern European countries once prohibited their citizens from buying photocopiers, the former Soviet Union used to ban civil use of international direct dial telephones, and some countries barred people from using short-wave radios. The results have been obvious.

China encompasses a vast territory and must depend on satellite television to see broadcasts from other cities, provinces, and autonomous regions. In remote regions and mountainous areas, local residents cannot receive the signals from Central China Television or from their own provincial television stations.

To offset the negative influence of overseas news, we must (1) make high-quality programming that will attract an audience,[12] (2) increase the freedom in our own reporting, thereby strengthening audience immunity against any detrimental effect of overseas news, and (3) develop and/or improve communication technology and the delivery of our programs.[13]

THE NEWS MEDIA AS AN INDUSTRY

Developing a market economy requires the news media to carry out significant reporting reforms, which will in turn require reform of news media practice and management. Fortunately, certain media outlets have already made some progress in this respect.

Reform of Organizational Structure and Division of Labor

Traditional beat coverage of governmental departments such as agriculture, industry, and transportation, and economic sectors such as metallurgy, energy, and textiles, has paralleled the operation of the planned economy. To accommodate the market economy, we need reporters to cover the stock exchanges, the futures markets, and special economic and development zones such as the Yangtze River Delta, the Pearl River Delta, and border trade zones.

Management Reform

At present, two-thirds of the nation's newspapers depend on government financial subsidies for survival. As part of the developing market economy and attendant press reform, all news media should stop "taking rice from the king" and evolve into legal entities responsible for their own profit and loss. Exceptions could be made for some highly specialized newspapers, some topical newspapers—for example, newspapers about family planning, education of the disabled, and environmental protection—and minority newspapers. Even those who enjoy subsidies should depend primarily on their own resources, both for the further development of their enterprise and the welfare of their employees. In general, the press industry should be market oriented, and news units should attach as much importance to management as to reporting. Managers should pay particular attention to such matters as business operations, advertising, and subscription sales.

Quality of Reporter Skills

News reporters should become more proficient and knowledgeable. In the past, many reporters covered the same ministry for a long time, typically publishing one article each month. As a result, their range of knowledge was narrow and their achievements were few.

In the future, the press industry will face new competition, both from the electronic media and between and among print publications. That competition will demand a sense of competition. Reporters will need to find the motivation to "rush for news," "struggle for timeliness," and work long, hard hours. The situation will also require public relations and computer skills. Reporters and editors will need a working knowledge of economics, and they will need to understand the law, both to ensure that their own reports comply with legal requirements and to avoid lawsuits from inaccurate reports. A new press industry under the market economy will produce many famous reporters, outstanding newspapermen and women, and excellent broadcasters.

MACROSCOPIC ADMINISTRATION OVER THE PRESS SECTOR

Propelled by the socialist market economy, the news media will multiply, information will increase, and press freedom will expand. It is therefore important to begin the gradual reform of the government's administration of the press industry and to establish new management structures. Although administrative and managerial reform should be based on the results of systematic testing, we can present a number of preliminary designs for discussion.

The Government's Administration of the Press Industry Should Be Macroscopic

First, the government should map out short-and long-term plans for the press industry, focusing on the growth of newspapers, radio stations, and television stations. Second, during this development period, the government should make frequent analyses and forecasts of various statistical trends, such as newspaper production, subscription sales, distribution, management structure, or the production, sales, and ownership of radio and television sets. The government should present its findings through the news media in the form of white papers. The government should also organize, coordinate, and support the creation, production, and application of new communication technologies.

To achieve government administration of the press according to law, the government should establish a press law, a broadcasting law, and rules governing news disputes and lawsuits.

SUMMARY

Temporary administrative directives to the press should gradually diminish, and all directives should be made as flexible and unintrusive as possible.

A Multi-level Administration Over the Press Industry Is Necessary

Party newspapers should be run according to decisions of Party committees and adhere to the Party's principles and standards of quality. Any demands and directives imposed on Party newspapers should be in keeping with the Constitution of China and with Party and group decisions made by Party committees. Flagrant interference from individuals should not be tolerated.

The Government Should Delegate More Administrative Authority Over the Press to Lower-level Agencies

For example, now that the concept of market competition has been accepted, the approval and registration of newspapers and magazines could be handled by provincial authorities, rather than by the central government. Registered newspapers could be allowed to increase the number of pages they publish without government approval. When state security interests or government or Party secrets are involved, administrative departments can conduct briefings for the appropriate news unit(s). Those briefings could introduce pertinent background and information and provide the opportunity to make suggestions or impose requirements.

Government Can Reinforce the Press in Disciplining Itself and Reward Model Journalists Who Abide by Professional Ethics

The government can help to establish meetings where the reporting of significant events can be constructively discussed. After all, the socialist market economy is under construction, and socialist press freedom is still developing.

How the press industry will operate in a market economy is still under discussion. What I have presented here are only immature opinions. It is the intention of this writing to elicit the valuable opinions of others and to arouse the interest of more intelligent people to participate in the discussion.

NOTES

1. Mao Zedong, "The period of bourgeois direction at The Wenhui Daily," *The People's Daily*. June 14, 1957.

2. Ibid.

3. *Selected Works from Deng Xiaoping* (1975–1982), pp. 287–88, People's Press, 1989.

4. Vice chairman of the Central Committee of the Chinese Communist Party.

5. December 1978.

6. In his preface to *A Critique of Political Economy*, Marx said, "In the social production of their life, men enter into definite relations of production which correspond to a definite stage of development of their material productive forces. The sum total of these relations of production constitutes the economic structure of society, the real foundation on which rises a legal and political superstructure and to which correspond definite forms of social consciousness." Karl Marx, *Selected Writings* (1985), ed. David McLellan, p. 389.

7. The first industry is agriculture; the second is manufacturing; the third is social services. Tying the news media to the "Three Industries" policy places them in a bureaucratic category that permits reform.

8. The term has become widely used to indicate China, Hong Kong, and the United States.

9. In 1992, Deng Xiaoping conducted a tour of inspection throughout Guandong and Hainan Provinces, during which he delivered many speeches promoting further development of his reform policy and open policy.

10. "Service" means that newspapers serve readers by providing relevant information; this is in addition to their existing mission of "guiding" readers in matters of policy, process, and regulation.

11. The General Agreement on Tariffs and Trade, has been replaced by the World Trade Organization.

12. The Zhujiang Economic Television Station retains a large audience share in a market that includes Hong Kong stations through its comprehensive program content and reform.

13. China is now developing a form of high-definition television.

CHAPTER 8 _____

China's Legal System Concerning Press Law

China's Constitution and a few scattered laws provide what legal authority exists on press-related issues. The Communist Party Propaganda Department and the State Press and Publication Administration—which provide the more specific, strict control—also formulate ongoing regulations. The press, however, hopes to have a discrete press law that not only defines the responsibilities and obligations of journalists but also protects their rights. This chapter was written in 1997 and revised in 1999.

THE THREE LAYERS OF THE LEGAL SYSTEM

At present, there is no specialized press law in China. The legal system under which the press operates refers to all the laws and regulations that standardize journalism and communication activities. Those regulations exist in three layers: (1) the Constitution; (2) all of the articles related to journalism and communication activities as they appear in various laws; and (3) specific regulations on newspapers, magazines, radio, and television.

Article 22 of the Constitution provides for the development and purpose of China's press: "The state promotes the development of art and literature, the press, radio and television broadcasting, publishing and distribution services, libraries, museums, cultural centers and other cultural undertakings that serve the people and socialism. . . ."[1]

Article 35 stipulates: "Citizens of the People's Republic of China enjoy freedom of speech, of the press, of assembly, of association, of procession and of demonstration."[2]

Article 38 affirms: "The personal dignity of citizens of the People's Republic of China is inviolable. Insult, libel, false accusation or false incrimination directed against citizens by any means is prohibited."[3]

And Article 53 says: "Citizens of the People's Republic of China must abide by the Constitution and the law [and] keep state secrets. . . ."[4]

Ostensibly based on the Constitution, certain laws also have provisions that affect journalism and communication activities. These laws include the Civil Law, the Criminal Law, the Law on Keeping National Secrets, the National Security Law, the Law on Copyrights, the Law on Advertisement, and the Law on Protection of Minors. The National Security Law,[5] for example, provides criminal sanctions for

plotting to subvert the government, dismember the state, or overthrow the socialist system; participating in foreign intelligence organizations or accepting missions from such organizations or their agents; stealing, probing, purchasing or unlawfully providing state secrets; instigating, bribing or luring state personnel to defect; and any other sabotage prejudicial to national security.[6]

The Criminal Law[7] similarly sanctions anyone who "instigates the subversion of the political power of the state and overthrows the socialist system through spreading rumors, slandering, or by other means . . ."[8] or "steals, secretly gathers, purchases, or illegally provides state secrets or intelligence for an organization, institution, or personnel outside the country. . . ."[9]

The Criminal Law also imposes sanctions on anyone caught intentionally "fabricating stories to frame others or in an attempt to subject others to criminal investigation"[10] or "openly insulting others using force or other methods or those fabricating stories to slander others."[11]

The Civil Law[12] provides that citizens and legal entities "shall enjoy the right of reputation. The personality of citizens shall be protected by the law, and the use of insults, libel or other means to damage the reputation of citizens or legal persons shall be prohibited."[13]

The Law on Protecting National Secrets[14] defines the scope of national secrets, the system that provides for their security, and the legal ramifications of leaking those secrets.

In addition to these laws, the Communist Party and government have formulated many special regulations to manage journalistic and communication activities. These regulations include the *Administration of*

Newspapers Provisional Rules[15] and the *Administration of Periodicals Provisional Rules*,[16] which contain detailed provisions for the establishment, approval, registration, publication, management, and penalties of newspapers and magazines. There are nearly 100 such regulations; among them, the *Decision on Improving Publishing Standards and Strengthening Controls on Publication*[17] (issued in 1983), the *Administration of Printing Businesses Provisional Regulations*[18] (issued in 1988), and the *Administration of Cable Television Regulations*[19] (issued in 1994).

THE LEGAL RESTRICTIONS ON NEWS SELECTION

Although the Constitution states that China's citizens enjoy the freedoms of speech and publication, most of the regulations deal with control and management of the press. Few stress the rights of the press. Although this emphasis on managing the press provides detailed direction for its control, even the most enlightened policies of the last ten years have yet to guarantee the freedom of speech and publication provided in the Constitution. Nowhere is the consequence of this imbalance more evident than in the restrictions imposed on news selection.

The selection of news should be decided according to news value and editorial policy, following the basic principles of journalism. This assertion enjoys wide support in principle, but in practice, China's media decided what to publish based on what is deemed beneficial to society. Anything deemed contrary to the Communist Party and the socialist system is banned. Most of the key press regulations are actually about which stories to encourage and which to forbid. Thus, to permit publication of a story means the system has determined that the content serves society; to ban a story means the system has determined that the content could engender negative effects.

As a result, the media in China are the tool of the propaganda establishment. The Newspaper Regulations say,

Newspapers in China, as an important part of the press led by the Communist Party must:

- adhere to the principles of serving the socialist system and the people;
- adhere to the principle of regarding social benefit as the highest standard;
- propagate Marxism, Leninism and the thought of Mao Zedong;
- propagate the policies of the Communist Party and the government;
- disseminate information and knowledge of science, technology and culture;
- provide the masses with healthy entertainment;
- reflect people's opinions and suggestions, and
- shoulder the responsibility of supervision.[20]

Of all these objectives, the highest is considered to be that of benefiting society. Propaganda is therefore considered newspapers' chief function, superior to the dissemination of information and supervision of the media.

This emphasis on the media's propaganda function is reasonable. China is a developing country. Its economy and technology lag behind other countries; the people's education is inadequate, and their understanding of democracy is weak. Using the media as a resource to develop the country and society is both laudable and necessary. For example, using the media's propaganda function to reform state-owned enterprises, ultimately benefits societal reform, development, and stability. Thus, reform of state-owned enterprises, a key to China's economic reform, will directly decide the fate of China's modernization drive. Therefore, coverage of that particular reform serves primarily to propagate the Party and government's reform policies, promote those enterprises that reform successfully, and so help other enterprises improve their own efficiency and avoid difficulty in implementing the reforms. The responsibility for reporting on problems created during the reform—such as strikes, demonstrations, and unemployment—belongs to internal reference publications.[21] In the current, difficult period, this system is both necessary and beneficial. If the media were to report problems fully and objectively, society could become unstable, and the instability could endanger reform.

However, restrictions on what the media may or may not cover should be limited to a few select issues and only during unusual periods. If restrictions are widely imposed over a long period of time, the media will lack variety and freedom, individual thought and insight will be smothered, and the sound policies of the Communist Party and the government will be derailed, as has happened repeatedly throughout China's history. For that reason, even as they enjoy full access to the media for the purpose of achieving socially beneficial reform, the Party and government must gradually increase press freedom.

Article 8 of the Newspaper Regulations provides that newspapers may not

- incite obstruction of or sabotage law enforcement;
- incite subversion of the socialist system;
- incite rebellion or riots;
- incite opposition to the leadership of the Chinese Communist Party;
- disclose state secrets;
- incite hostility and ill feeling among different races;
- incite sabotage of social order and stability;
- propagate indecency, obscenity, violence, superstition, or pseudo science, or defame or humiliate others.[22]

The intent of both propaganda and content restrictions is to control the selection of news and maximize social benefit. Implementation of these regulations is a crucial issue. Overemphasizing the importance of a story's benefit to society can limit the media's freedom just as surely as prohibiting certain coverage. Both can have dire consequences.

The Qiandao Lake event of March 31, 1994, in Zhejiang Province is one such instance. Three criminals hijacked a cruise boat on Qiandao Lake. They robbed the passengers and then burned the boat. All thirty-two passengers and crew members were killed, including twenty-four tourists from Taiwan. Because this event involved relations with Taiwan, all news reports were banned. Not until April 10 did Xinhua News Agency run a story about the tragedy. The incident was purely a criminal one, but the media were not allowed to cover it, leaving overseas media to wonder what really happened. The lack of solid news allowed rumors to spread quickly. The rumors were exploited by anti-Communists, and the ensuing false stories ultimately exacerbated tensions on both sides of the Taiwan Straits.

MANAGING THE LEGAL SYSTEM GOVERNING THE PRESS

In China, Party propaganda departments control the ideology of the press. The Agency of Media and Publications and its provincial sub-bureaus control administrative management. Administration takes three forms.

The Media Registration System

The administrative agencies have the authority to approve new media outlets. To start a new newspaper requires two permits: one from the governing department and one from the Agency of Media and Publications. Once approved, registered and licensed, the newspaper can be published; otherwise, it is regarded as illegal and will be banned. Article 10 of the Newspaper Regulations provides that every new newspaper must have "fixed and competent sponsoring and supervisory units within government."[23] In other words, it is impossible for individuals or private groups to launch media outlets in China.

Administrative Agencies Have the Right to Manage the Media's Daily Operations

To control the quality of newspapers and magazines, the Agency of Media and Publications had devised regulations on proofreading. Proofreaders check whether or not the magazines and newspapers carry out Party policy. In 1995, the Agency of Media and Publications drafted quality control standards by which to evaluate any given newspaper's editorial policy, content, printing, advertising, and even circulation. Newspapers that cannot meet these standards are shut down. The Ministry of Radio and Television also has a proofreading system.

In June 1993, the Agency of Media and Publications worked out the *Responsibilities of the Sponsoring Unit and Supervisory Unit of Publishing Units Provisional Regulations.*[24] It provides that "the relationship between the media's supervisory department and the media itself is that of the leader and the led." The supervisory departments are expected to

lead and supervise the media in abiding by Party policy and strategy, the government's laws, regulations and policies, and the media's editing policy and reporting focus; examine the media's important news coverage and topic selections and approve the publication of important works (books, editorials and reports); decide whether or not to circulate its publications; and be responsible for mistakes in the publications and other problems.

Topics being considered for publication must be submitted for approval. The *Notice on Some Topics that Need Special Approval* (issued in June 1988) required that topics concerning senior officials of the Nationalist Party and such historical figures as Chen Duxiu, Wang Ming, and Zhang Guotao[25] should be submitted to an upper-level department for approval. The *Regulation on Publishing Books on the Cultural Revolution* stipulates in principle that reference books, novels, memoirs, biographies, and nonfiction stories about the Cultural Revolution will not be published. Such regulations also include the *Notice on Strengthening the Management of Publications Concerning the Soviet Union and East European Countries* (issued in June 1990) and the *Regulation on Strengthening the Management of Publications on Senior Party and Government Officials* (issued in May 1990).

Administrative Agencies Have the Right to Punish the Media for Their Illegal Activities

Such punishments include warnings, fines, confiscating illegal income and publications, and canceling licenses. In April 1997, the Agency of Media and Publications punished eight publishing companies for printing bad books and selling book publishing permits. Of the eight, three publishing companies, including the Inner Mongolia Audio and Video Publishing Company, were shut down; the other five were reorganized.

SOME PRESS-RELATED LAWS ARE IN LINE WITH INTERNATIONAL PRACTICE

There is a vast difference between China and Western countries in their systems of law, news selection, and press management. Some laws in China are quite similar to their Western counterparts, however, including the laws on copyrights and advertising and the regulations on libel.

Article 94 of the Civil Law provides: "Citizens and legal persons shall enjoy rights of authorship (copyrights) and shall be entitled to sign their names as authors, issue and publish their works, and obtain remuneration in accordance with the law."[26] The 118th article stipulates: "Citizens and legal persons have the right to ask for protection and compensation if their copyrights, patents, trademarks, rights of discovery, rights of invention and other scientific and technological achievement are infringed by plagiarizing, alteration and imitation."

Article 2 of the Law on Copyrights provides:

Works of Chinese citizens, legal entities or entities without legal personality, whether published or not, shall enjoy copyright in accordance with this law. Works of foreigners first published in the territory of the People's Republic of China shall enjoy copyright in accordance with this law. Any work of a foreigner published outside the territory of the People's Republic of China which is eligible to enjoy copyright under an agreement concluded between the country to which the foreigner belongs and China, or under an international treaty to which both countries are party, shall be protected in accordance with this law.[27]

In addition to the Civil Law and the Law on Copyrights, the Chinese government has begun taking measures to ensure that copyrights will be well protected in China.

The Advertisement Law is fairly comprehensive, outlining the parameters for advertising content, management, operation, and punishment.[28]

The Constitution and other laws also have provisions on slander and defamation. In addition to the articles in the Constitution mentioned above, related provisions exist in the Criminal Law, the Civil Law, the Regulation on Security Management, and the Law on Protection of Minors. These laws and regulations have been well implemented.

A typical application is the case of Xi Hong, a trade union official in Xinjiang Uighur Autonomous Region, who accused *The People's Daily* of impugning her reputation. On July 20, 1988, *The People's Daily* ran a story criticizing Xi for slow work and for spreading untrue stories about other people at her work site. Xi believed she had been slandered, and in October, she sued *The People's Daily* in the People's Court of Chaoyang District in Beijing. The case was accepted in March 1989, but *The People's Daily* did not respond until 1992, and the case was repeatedly postponed. Xi was repeatedly asked to settle, but she pressed on for a trial. In January 1997, Xi agreed to the paper's most recent offer and received an apology and 20,000 yuan in compensation.

CONCLUSION

China's laws and regulations stress that the press should adhere to Communist Party principles, emphasize the positive aspects of any given story, regard benefit to society as the highest of editorial standards, and consider a story's domestic and overseas ramifications. These are the defining characteristics of China's press. The press is still largely regarded as a part of the Communist Party's propaganda agency, and its freedom has been restricted.

As to the laws and regulations themselves, contradictions exist between the Constitution and policy regulations. The progressive, solemn, high standards found in the articles of the Constitution contrast sharply with the antiquated, random, low standards of the Party and government regulations. The latter contain detailed provisions concerning press obligations, whereas its rights are seldom mentioned.

Some press rights have yet to be defined by the legal system. For example, the concept of a free press is never mentioned, and there are as yet no laws or regulations to protect the right of reporting and interviewing. The result of these contradictions is that the Constitution is put on the shelf while various arbitrary regulations control the press. This happens when power replaces the law and democracy is slow to progress.

There also remains a considerable gap between regulation and implementation. Law is necessarily difficult to enforce in a society whose legal system is incomplete. In the current system, a reporter who has accurately cited an article to show that his report is legal could still be accused of having written a story detrimental to society on the premise that the story was not in line with the Propaganda Department's intention. Since the right to judge whether the social effect is beneficial or detrimental does not belong to the reporter and the press, the reporter would probably be criticized or even punished.

China's economic, cultural, and political reforms are progressing rapidly. Surely, the ongoing construction of democracy and the legal system will proceed. Devising a press law to protect socialist freedom of the press is both in the interest of the proletariat and in keeping with the inevitable direction of history.

NOTES

1. Constitution of the People's Republic of China, adopted at the Fifth Session of the Fifth National People's Congress and promulgated for implementation by the Proclamation of the National People's Congress on December 4, 1982. English translation from *The Laws of the People's Republic of China, 1979–1982*, compiled by the Legislative Affairs Commission of the Standing Committee of the National

People's Congress of the People's Republic of China, Foreign Languages Press, Beijing, 1987.

2. Ibid.

3. Ibid.

4. Ibid.

5. Promulgated by the Standing Committee of the National People's Congress on February 22, 1993. See H. L. Fu and Richard Cullen, *Media Law in the PRC*, Asia Law and Practice Publishing Ltd., 1996, pp. 109–135 (hereinafter Fu & Cullen).

6. Fu & Cullen, 133, paraphrasing the PRC National Security Law, Article 4.

7. Criminal Law of the People's Republic of China. Adopted by the Second Session of the Fifth National People's Congress on July 1, 1979, and amended by the Fifth Session of the Eighth National People's Congress on March 14, 1997. English translation, Charles D. Paglee, Chinalaw Web, PRC Criminal Law, http://www.qis.net/chinalaw/prclaw60.htm (hereinafter, Criminal Law).

8. Criminal Law, Art. 105.

9. Criminal Law, Art. 111.

10. Criminal Law, Art. 243.

11. Criminal Law, Art. 246.

12. General Principles of the Civil Law of the People's Republic of China, adopted at the Fourth Session of the Sixth National People's Congress, promulgated by Order No. 37 of the president of the People's Republic of China on April 12, 1986, and effective as of January 1, 1987. English translation from *The Laws of the People's Republic of China, 1979–1982*, compiled by the Legislative Affairs Commission of the Standing Committee of the National People's Congress of the People's Republic of China, Foreign Languages Press, Beijing, 1987.

13. Civil Law, Art. 101.

14. Adopted by the National People's Congress in May 1988. See Fu & Cullen, p. 109 et seq.

15. Adopted by the Agency of Media and Publications, December 25, 1990. See Fu & Cullen, p. 31 et seq. (hereinafter, Newspaper Regulations).

16. Adopted by the AMP in 1988.

17. See Fu & Cullen, p. 60.

18. Ibid.

19. Ibid, 85.

20. Supra, note 15, pp. 34–35.

21. These internal journals exist within every department.

22. Supra, note 15.

23. Supra, note 15, p. 31.

24. Adopted June 29, 1993. See Fu & Cullen, p. 31.

25. Some of the original founding revolutionary leaders who are no longer venerated.

26. Civil Law, Art. 94.

27. Copyright Law of People's Republic of China, adopted at the Fifteenth Session of the Standing Committee of the Seventh National People's Congress on September 7, 1990. English translation provided by the National Copyright Administration of China. See Charles D. Paglee, Chinalaw Web, PRC Copyright Law, http://www.qis.net/chinalaw/lawtran1.htm (hereinafter, Copyright Law).

28. Advertisements Law of the People's Republic of China, adopted at the tenth session of the Standing Committee of the Eighth National People's Congress on October 27, 1994, circulated by Order No. 34 of the president of the People's Republic of China on October 27, 1994, and effective as of February 1, 1995. See Charles D. Paglee, Chinalaw Web, PRC Advertisements Law, http://www.qis.net/chinalaw/lawtran1.htm (hereinafter, Copyright Law).

_____

CHAPTER 9

The Difficulty of Writing Press Legislation in China

Western press laws have historically been difficult to draft. Both the press and society have feared that a press law could restrict press freedom.[1] Drafting China's press law has also been difficult, but for a much different reason: government officials worry that such a law will prevent them from controlling the press. The author has written about this issue since the early 1980s. This treatment was written in 1997, specifically for this book.

CHRONICLE OF A PRESS LAW

More than eighteen years have passed since the deputies in the 1980 National People's Congress (NPC) first proposed designing a press law for China, and there is still no such legislation in sight. A chronicle of China's attempts at drafting press legislation may explain both the problems in that process and in the system itself.

1978

During the ten-year Cultural Revolution, from 1966 to 1976, China's journalists were denied the freedom to tell the truth. Two years after the

Cultural Revolution ended, members of the press suggested drafting a press law to safeguard each citizen's freedom of speech and publication.

1980

During the 1980 National People's Congress, deputies from the press officially proposed formulating a press law.

1983

Three years later, the June meeting of the sixth National People's Congress formally agreed to "draft the Press Law of the People's Republic of China when conditions have matured."[2]

1984

In January 1984, the press bureau of the Party's Propaganda Ministry approved the establishment of a committee to draft such a law. The group, headed by Hu Jiwei and composed of individuals from the press and legal communities, was organized by the NPC Committee on Education, Science, and Culture.[3] More than five years after the first proposal, work on China's press legislation had formally begun.

1984–85

The NPC committee's first work was to form a research department on press law. That department, headed by the author and made up of research fellows and media law graduate students, chronicled its work in the new *Journal of Press Law*. The committee seminars that were held in Beijing, Shanghai, Guangzhou, Chengdu, and Chongqing provided discussion forums for the country's press and law experts. A Shenzhen meeting solicited advice from Hong Kong journalists. The research department completed a first draft within that first year.[4]

The central government's immediate response to the press law research department's work was to assign the same task to another body. A similar cross-section of researchers in Shanghai was asked to prepare an entirely new "second draft."

1987

In 1987, the central government decided to form a third group—the State Press and Publication Administration—to oversee the project. This group also offered its draft of the press law. Later that year, the thirteenth National Congress of the Communist Party issued a general directive to expedite the process on the press and publication law.[5]

1994

The Central Committee of the Communist Party approved consideration of a press and publication law to be part of the 1994 NPC plan of suggested legislation. But Party officials in the Propaganda Ministry opposed renewed discussion of a press law per se on the grounds that press legislation was detrimental to both the Party and government. Such legislation, they maintained, had wrought havoc in the Soviet Union and Eastern Europe.[7]

If this progress is any indication, a Chinese press law will not be ready by the turn of the century.

WHY PRESS LAW IS OPPOSED

In the early 1980s through the early 1990s, leaders were eager to have a press law because they believed that a runaway press was more dangerous than a runaway economy. During those years, press coverage had been straying from Party policy (as when, during the 1989 political disturbances in Beijing, writers at *The People's Daily* and other media expressed tolerance and sympathy toward the demonstrators). The press had also secured a degree of autonomy as a result of a sudden expansion in news space, news outlets, and the kinds of articles that were permitted. The leadership believed that a press law would facilitate better control of the press.

As Party officials discovered more about the press law, however, they realized that it would not be a government tool to control the press. They realized that a press law would not only define press responsibilities and obligations, but would also safeguard press and citizen rights to free speech and publication as provided in the Constitution. Any specific definition of these rights would naturally impede the Propaganda Department's arbitrary interference with the press.

Drafting a press law is difficult work. The rights that must be defined include the people's right to a free press, their right to a "watchdog" press, and their right to launch new media. To understand what must be defined is to understand how profoundly difficult the process is.

DEFINING THE FREEDOMS

Defining the Rights of a Free Press

A free press is guaranteed in the Constitution, which also protects citizens' freedom of speech and publication. For that reason, protecting those freedoms has been central to each draft of China's press law.

Article 35 of the Constitution provides: "Citizens of the People's Republic of China enjoy freedom of speech, of the press, of assembly, of association, of procession and of demonstration."[8] There are no other provisions on freedom of speech, so the definition of freedom of speech and publication is unclear. The constitutional guarantee has never been cited as legal defense, nor do authoritative books in China elaborate upon it. However, this same premise is a fundamental tenet of many of the world's constitutions, including those of France, Germany, Italy, Sweden, and Belgium. Portugal's 1976 constitution has 317 words on the subject; the 1927 Greek constitution, 358 words; and in a 1974 amendment, Turkey's constitution gives the issue 1,000 words.[9] Some of the provisions are very specific.

Because China's Constitution has no such specific provisions for freedom of speech and publication, a press law to define those rights becomes even more critical. It is both scientific and rational for a press law to stipulate that "the media can disseminate any information and opinions that do not violate the Constitution." But such a rational premise cannot operate in a system in which a substantial percentage of news and information is banned because of its proported "bad social influence," or where opinions deemed to be "in violation of Party policy" cannot be published. It is also scientific and rational for a press law to stipulate that journalists should be subject only to those agencies whose power over them is authorized by law,[10] yet China's journalists must answer to myriad arbitrary restrictions and criticisms, few of which are based on law.

Defining the Media's Supervisory ("Watchdog") Role

In 1987, when the thirteenth National Party Congress specifically supported the media's supervisory function, it appeared that the door was open to include that function in the new press law. At issue, however, was how to define the "watchdog" function. One cannot rely upon an undefined right.

In theory, a press law should stipulate that, except in matters of national security, "the media have the right to report and comment on the ruling Party's and the government's decision-making process." The rhetoric of the thirteenth National Party Congress agreed, stressing that "[people should be] informed about important events; important issues should be discussed." But this emphasis is not being implemented. Except for a very few cases,[11] most decision-making processes have not been reported. For example, press legislation has been discussed for nearly twenty years, yet the draft of the law has never been publicized. Nor have people been allowed to express their opinions through the media.[12]

A press law that provides that "the media may publish criticism of any people or events that violate the Constitution and law" is in full accord with Article 41 of the Constitution, which guarantees that "Citizens of the People's Republic of China have the right to criticize or make suggestions to any government department or its staff." As it is now, Party newspapers may take issue only with those government departments that are considered to be at a lower level than the papers themselves[13]—in most cases, only common citizens and/or clerks.

Media supervision of Party, government, and senior officials has never existed in China. That is why the reasonable provision "The media may publish criticism of any people or events that violate the Constitution and other laws" remains unacceptable to Party and government officials. In fact, the people who object to the media fulfilling their "watchdog" function hope that a law concerning the press will actually protect senior Party and government officials *from* media criticism.

Defining the Right to Launch a Publication

If the Constitution grants citizens the freedom to publish, then citizens should have the right to set up publishing houses and media outlets. But in China, all media belong to the state; all are state assets. Even though the trade union, the youth league, and the women's association have initiated their own special interest newspapers, these newspapers are still controlled by the Party branches of these organizations, and all of their staffs are state workers. There are no private media in China.

One of the main criticisms of the research committee's initial press law draft was its stance on freedom to publish. The wording was clear: "Individuals can launch newspapers and periodicals."[14] Officials who read that draft disapproved, and the freedom was omitted. As of now, only state-owned entities can launch publications. The wording of this provision was later modified, but the content remains the same: publications can be launched only by the state, not by individuals or private groups.

How, then, can the freedom to publish be expressed? Legal experts have asked the same question. The quandary is one of the reasons the publication law is still on the shelf.

Undoubtedly, if the media had the benefit of the three rights mentioned above, media freedom in China would markedly improve, and the relationship between the Communist Party and the media would fundamentally change. In the final analysis, the three dilemmas meet at one point: managing the relationship between the Communist Party and the media. At the beginning of the drafting process, it was made clear that "The press law should not be too specific; the law should not limit the Party's control over the media."

COULD A LAW THAT CONTROLS THE PRESS BE PASSED

The traditional role of the media in China is that of Party and government mouthpiece. As such, the media are expected to abide by Party leadership and adhere to its policies and principles. Then, in keeping with that traditional role and its advocates, why not write that into the press law? Because it cannot be legislated.

The Constitution stipulates, "All . . . political parties and public organizations . . . must abide by the Constitution and the law."[15] The Communist Party has to abide by laws based on the Constitution. A press law could never ensure the Party's autonomous right to random, strict control and management of the press, even if such control might sometimes benefit national interest.

Until now, it has not been possible to circumvent the difficulties of articulating media rights, and—because of existing written and unwritten regulations that already control and manage the press—neither is it crucial for the Party and government to promote a discrete press law. Clearly, press legislation in China still has a long way to go.

A POSSIBLE SOLUTION: DIFFERENTIATE BETWEEN PARTY AND NON-PARTY PRESS

In the end, however, effective Party leadership and press legislation are not incompatible. The two can coexist if we clearly differentiate between two entities: the Party's press and the country's press. In 1994, the author wrote: "The *Party's press* refers to the Party's newspapers. But news agencies, radio and TV stations and newspapers, as a whole, should be called the country's press or the *people's press*. This differentiation offers a workable distinction between Party and non-Party press and overcomes the impasse of press management."[16]

"The management of the press should be organized around a two-tiered standard: (1) the legal standard, answering only to the Constitution and law (which would need to include a press law) and (2) the Party standard, under which Party newspapers would have to abide not only by the Constitution and laws, but also follow the Party's decisions and policies."[17] In other words, the press law would govern the press's legal relations with the country and the society, whereas the Party would have jurisdiction over its own newspapers. The Party would still be able to offer its perspective to the non-Party press, but as counsel, not rule. Thus the Party leadership could rest assured that its central position in political life and the Party newspapers would remain intact. In this way, the Party's voice and policies would be transmitted by Party newspapers, the general press system could enjoy ample freedom, and the obstacles to press legislation discussed above would be surmounted.

NOTES

1. Such was the case in Germany, France, Australia, Canada, and elsewhere.
2. Sun Xupei was to be heavily involved in the drafting effort. See Won Ho Chang, *Mass Media in China*, Iowa University Press, 1989.

3. *Journal of the Press Law* 1, p. 4, 1984, compiled by the Research Department on Press Law. Hu Jiwei was the vice director of the NPC Committee on Education, Science, and Culture at that time.

4. *Journal of the Press Law* 4, p. 16–22, 1985.

5. See Lynn T. White III, "All the News: Structure and Politics in Shanghai's Reform Media," in *Voices of China: The Interplay of Politics and Journalism*, Chin-Chuan Lee, ed., The Guilford Press, 1990.

6. With the political unrest of 1989, including the Tienanmen Square incident, little was done on the press law. Some people toyed with it, but nothing substantive was changed or added. See Judy Polumbaum, "The Tribulations of China's Journalists after a Decade of Reform," in *Voices of China: The Interplay of Politics and Journalism*, Chin-Chuan Lee, ed., The Guilford Press, 1990.

7. This argument was articulated by a government official at a national journalism education conference.

8. Constitution of the People's Republic of China, adopted at the Fifth Session of the Fifth National People's Congress and promulgated for implementation by the Proclamation of the National People's Congress on December 4, 1982. Translation in *The Laws of the People's Republic of China, 1979–1982*, compiled by the Legislative Affairs Commission of the Standing Committee of the National People's Congress of the People's Republic of China.

9. The Chinese often justify the importance of an idea according to how many "characters" have been written about it; hence, the enumeration of words.

10. See, e.g., Article 3 of Egypt's press law: "Journalists are independent persons who are not restricted by non-law powers in their work." *The Collection of Other Countries' Press and Publication Laws*, p. 143, People's Daily Publishing House, 1981.

11. As when the media openly reported the discussion and design process of the Bankruptcy Law.

12. For example, the media were not allowed to publish viewpoints that opposed construction of the Three Gorges Dam on the Yangtze River.

13. In March 1953, *The Yishan Farmers News* criticized the Yishan Party committee, the paper's governing entity. The newspaper was subsequently criticized by the Guangxi and Central Government propaganda departments. As a result, the Propaganda Ministry ordered: "[A] Party newspaper has no right to oppose its Party committee." *The Dictionary of Journalism*, compiled by Gan Xifen, Henan People's Publishing House, 1993.

14. *Journal of the Press Law* 20, p. 4, 1988.

15. Article 5.

16. Sun Xupei, *New Theory on Journalism*, p. 132, Modern China Publishing House, 1994.

17. "Research Outline on the Reform of the Press System," *Journal of the Press Law* 19, p. 3, 1987.

_____

CHAPTER 10

The Individual's Right to Reputation and the Press's Right to Report

In 1987, China implemented its General Principles of Civil Law, which provide legal protection for the reputation of citizens, organizations, and other entities. The principles have proved a challenge to the traditional standards of China's official newspapers. Following the implementation of the General Principles of Civil Law, defamation lawsuits involving China's press rapidly increased. How should we deal with this situation? Which of our journalism practices no longer suit a society run by law? Must we be careful to balance protecting citizens' rights to reputation even as we protect the media's right to report the news? These questions were the subject of the following article, first drafted in 1993 and updated in 1997.

HOW SHOULD WE INTERPRET THE RISE IN LAWSUITS AGAINST THE PRESS?

The General Principles of Civil Law of the People's Republic of China took effect on January 1, 1987. The principles stipulate that "Citizens and legal persons shall enjoy the right of reputation. The personality of citizens shall be protected by law, and the use of insults, libel or other means to damage the reputation of citizens or legal persons shall be prohibited."[1] Since then, defamation suits against the press have rapidly increased. Charges targeting reporters, newspapers, and magazines are common not only in China's major cities, but also in the remote areas of Xinjiang, Inner Mongolia, and Guangxi autonomous regions. By the end of May 1997, more than a thousand lawsuits had been lodged nationwide. The following statistics from Shanghai, Beijing, and the nation suggest that the total number could be larger still.

Shanghai: "From the day the General Principles of Civil Law took effect to March 1990, the People's Courts of Shanghai accepted and heard 40 defamation lawsuits against the news industry."[2] But cases heard far exceeded that number. During that period, Shanghai's Huangpu District alone "heard 72 civil lawsuits against news reports."[3]

Beijing: "From 1987 to the end of 1992, different levels of the Beijing People's Courts heard 220 cases on disputes concerning harm to reputation, constituting roughly 85 per cent of all personal rights violation cases (which include cases involving infringement of a person's, product's, or organization's right to the use of their name and likeness)." Among the defamation cases, "27.7 per cent have . . . been against the news industry."[4]

The nation: "Statistics available to date show that during the first half of 1988, China's courts accepted and heard more than 200 news-related disputes and lawsuits."[5]

According to related statistics: the percentage of reputation damage cases among the total number of cases heard by courts of different levels across China was 20 per cent in 1989, an increase of 10.2 per cent over the previous year. Such cases reached 1,697 in number during the first nine months of 1990, increasing by 10.34 per cent over the same period in 1989. These news-related infringement cases make up approximately 10 per cent of the total reputation dispute cases. Among China's regions, Shanghai witnessed the vast majority of such cases.[6]

Looking at the Issue from Different Perspectives

The increase in defamation suits against the press cannot be simplistically classified as good or bad. To fully understand this situation, it must be analyzed from different perspectives.

The legal perspective

First, from a legal perspective, the situation reflects the Chinese people's rising awareness of law and greater degree to which they value the protection of human dignity. People are now more likely to refer to the law and, subsequently, to turn to the courts when they believe their reputations have been impugned. Civil defamation cases in particular increased after the issuance of the General Principles of Civil Law in

1987, which provide the legal remedy for harm to reputation. Because no civil law existed before that, few civil disputes were heard.

From the larger perspective, this phenomenon is commensurate with the development of China's legal system and the implementation of rule by law. The large number of lawsuits thrown out by the courts demonstrates continued misunderstanding of the law, as individuals, unable to discriminate between normal media supervision and disparagement of reputation, have brought inappropriate charges. Also among the latter group were cases in which "the guilty party filed"—someone intentionally brought charges against the media in an attempt to appear victimized and so offset proper and justifiable media criticism.

The media's perspective

The cases show that a considerable number of journalists do not understand how to work in a way that avoids dispute and lawsuit. For example, in two cases in the late 1980s, reporters were convicted of slander in criminal court.[7] Defendants in both cases were given criminal sanctions, and in both cases, the defendants refused to accept several attempts at mediation. They either thought they were safe because, even though the articles each targeted a specific person, their articles did not use the subject's real name,[8] or they naively assumed they could hide behind a blind assertion that they had never heard of legal consequences for unsubstantiated criticism!

In another example, an indignant journalist told the following story: "My hometown newspaper published a criticism article that misrepresented certain facts, causing the subject only minor injury to his reputation. The man brought charges, and the newspaper was ultimately required to give him 200 yuan in settlement! What a ridiculous state of affairs!" That journalist still considers the mediating of a solution as evidence of moral deterioration.

After the "June 4" event in 1989, the central government required all propaganda organs to devote most of their space to "positive reports."[9] Immediately, there was significant decline in both critical reporting and in lawsuits against the press. It should be pointed out that the effect may have been due in part to a growing understanding of the conditions, causes, and effects of defamation.

Xu Xun, a veteran reporter of court news, has divided press-related court actions after 1988 into three phases:

According to my observation, 1988 was the first peak year of China's press lawsuits, when plaintiffs were in large part common citizens, and Shanghai was the center for such cases ... The second crest of news-related lawsuits was 1992, when plaintiffs were for the most part artists, and the center was Beijing ... In mid-1993, while the repercussions of the second peak were still in effect, the third peak manifested itself in more corporate defamation suits against the press.[10]

With the plethora of lawsuits against the news industry and with newspapers declaring such grievances "in fashion," Chinese courts have implemented a principle of "whoever files suit must also supply evidence." They are generally prudent as to which cases will be heard and refuse to accept cases with insufficient evidence. In 1988—during the first phase of such litigation—Shanghai litigants brought fifty-eight news-related defamation lawsuits, of which only twenty-one (36.8 percent) were accepted and heard by the courts.

During the three years after the issuance of the General Principles of Civil Law, Shanghai's Huangpu District alone[11] considered seventy-two such cases, of which—after investigation by appropriate government branches and out-of-court settlements—only ten (13.8 percent) were ultimately heard. Many such press disputes are now resolved out of court.

Surely, too strict a limitation on initiating lawsuits could violate citizens' legal rights. On the other hand, China is only now beginning to implement mass media law, and both journalists and the public still lack understanding of media law. For that reason, imposing certain necessary limitations will not only forestall specious lawsuits and reduce the burden on the courts, but will also reduce the harassment suffered by the mass media and reporters. Sensible restrictions can even minimize or eliminate loss to the plaintiffs.

DEFINING INFRINGEMENT

According to the *China Encyclopedia on Law*, infringement can be thought of as having four conditions:

1. *Injury exists.* Injury refers to losses in assets or personal injury caused by the one who carries out the action toward the one who suffers damage.

2. *The action that led to the injury is illegal.* This means that the actor has to bear civil responsibility only when the action leading to the damage breaks the law. For example, some newspapers carry a column called *Moral Court*, which covers such stories as conflicts between father and son or wife and mother-in-law. Often, the column intensifies the antagonism. Although the reports themselves might be accurate, they infringe upon citizens' privacy. Therefore, they do not qualify as decent media supervision and so should bear civil responsibility.

3. *There is a causal factor linking the infringing action and the damages.* This means that the infringement causes the damage. When the damage results from more than one cause, it is necessary to differentiate between the primary and subsidiary causes. For instance, in one case a news report's depiction of unhealth-

ful conditions in a restaurant was inaccurate. After the article was published, business fell off sharply. Although the characterization of the restaurant as unacceptably unclean might have played a part in the drop-off, the main reason for the sharp decline proved to be that many nearby buildings had been bulldozed, and the neighborhood clientele moved away. Sometimes, news stories have the potential to cause only injury, but are not necessarily the reason for the inevitable damage that results. Thus, it is necessary to differentiate correlation from cause.

4. *The person/entity who causes the damage is at fault.* Some reports are simply edited government or judicial documents. Insofar as the report is faithful to the original document, even if the report causes injury to some person involved, neither the reporter nor the media can be regarded as having acted irresponsibly.

Only when all of the four elements exist can we say that an infringement case will stand. Therefore, if someone who raises a charge fails to supply evidence for one or more of the above elements, the court has sufficient reason to ask that the charge be withdrawn.[12]

Of course, the practice of reducing the number of lawsuits accepted by the court is intended to address China's legal situation at present, and it is probably a phenomenon peculiar to the Chinese way of doing things. As legal knowledge in China is disseminated throughout society, and as that society is increasingly run according to law, the abuse of lawsuits will sharply decrease. In time, the courts may be able to accept and hear all such lawsuits.

A MORE ACCURATE EXPLANATION FOR THE CHiNESE MEDIA'S TENDENCY TO DEFAME

The roots to the growth of lawsuits against the press since 1987 are even deeper and deserve serious research. With the founding of the People's Republic of China, the country implemented a completely different news system. As the mouthpiece of the Communist Party and the government, the media played a central role in the country's political and social life. The concept of "press lawsuits" and "infringement disputes" was nonexistent. For the next thirty years or so, feature news—which was considered "bourgeois"—was excluded from proletarian papers. Therefore, the potential for press infringement of reputation and privacy was negligible.

The Third Plenary Session of the Eleventh Central Committee of the Chinese Communist Party in 1978 marked the beginning of a new era of reform. It also ushered in a new era of legislation. The Constitution's admonition that all government agencies must abide by the Constitution and the law made it immediately apparent that the media, including both Party and non-Party newspapers, must produce news according to the law. It followed that any newspaper that broke the law should be punished according to the law.

While this reform was taking place, the journalism industry itself was undergoing major changes. To meet the needs of the burgeoning readership, newspapers added general society content to what had been strictly government-and Party-sponsored reports. Since such stories are more personal by nature, the likelihood of injury to reputation and privacy increased as well.

THREE APHORISMS THAT PREVENT JOURNALISM FROM ADJUSTING TO OPEN REFORM

Our journalists have yet to comprehend the critical need to adjust to this new era of legal reform with parallel reforms in journalistic practice. Three long-standing aphorisms continue to paralyze journalists and keep them from moving forward in the process of legal reform.

Thinking of the Mass Media as an Arm of Party and Government Power

Among the most enduring of the outmoded opinions is the regard for China's news media as authorities in their own right, as if they were guns or cannon. Were that the case, infringement upon the legal rights of various political and social organizations and citizens would be almost certain.

The question is, in a system of reform, are news media power organs or public opinion organs? Unquestionably, the news media are channels meant to transmit fact and opinion. They are also a channel for public opinion and information. At times, modern news media do wield considerable influence, but that is a form of mental strength, or "strength of sense," as Marx said, rather than political power.

However, the role of China's mass media has been blurred. For a number of years, society recognized our Party newspaper to be an actual Party department. So it seemed that whatever power the Party had was likewise conferred upon Party newspapers. Since the Party is the ruling party, it has seemed that Party newspapers have had governing power as well. In other words, because newspapers are Party newspapers, their power has seemed to equal that of the government organs behind them. A popular saying called newspapers the "invisible director and commander," and so, perceived as *commander* rather than *dispatcher*, newspapers seemed to acquire actual power of command.

The correlation emerged in revolutionary times when "guns and pens" were used in the struggle to wrest political power. However, it is important now to realize that it would have been impossible to establish systematic legislation at that time. Nor was it possible to plan comprehensive yet flexible political-control mechanisms. Hence, commanding through newspapers became the modus operandi.

The Soviet Union's news model, which we copied for many years, operated that way. In June 1922, the Central Committee of the Russian Communist Party wrote a letter to local, provincial, and central Party groups: "Editorials and other important opinion articles [of the Soviet Party newspapers] should lead and guide and be able to point out basic principles of behavior. Editorials and brief comments should not be informal viewpoints or discussions, but should be political instruction and decree."[13]

This system suited the needs of the revolutionary years. But once the People's Republic of China had been established and the various Party, government, legislative, and judicial mechanisms were in place, newspapers no longer needed to play a part in political power. Newspapers should have returned to their roles as public opinion organs. For various reasons, that transition did not take place.

The original Party and government attitude toward such a transition was clear. On October 30, 1949, the Central Propaganda Ministry and Xinhua News Agency issued an instruction:

Things within the scope of the central government should be discussed and decided by the government, and the decision should be made public directly by the government for implementation . . . For the same reason, from now on, editorials, comments and news analysis in the Party newspapers throughout China should take care not to use administrative attitudes and tones, and instead assume the attitude and tone of appealing, advising and discussing. Newspapers' assuming administrative attitudes and tones is not only an error at present, but also an error of the past.[14]

The paragraph was unambiguous in the role newspapers should play. However, these informed opinions were not carried out in the Leftist atmosphere that was to follow.[15]

Some might ask whether the media did not benefit from holding on to power. Personally, I think too much power contradicts the nature of the news media. The news media is a tool that provides information and transmits opinion. The information base and opinion market thus created facilitates the effective operation of all political power organs. Party newspapers, in particular, also disseminate Party and government policy and opinion; they should publish orders—laws, regulations, and other documents—but should not themselves issue orders. Nor should their opinions "assume the attitude and tone of administrative order."[16]

If the press aspires to power it does not rightfully possess, it assumes burdens it should not have to bear. Ultimately, that press forfeits its basic freedom, even as it muddles legislation and political interests. History has proven it so.

Admittedly, China's mass media have functioned beyond their purview for a long time. In 1967, just as the highest echelons of the Party and central government were poised to make a decision on economic reform, newspapers published articles heaping criticism on "the biggest capitalist representatives within the Communist Party," and slandered President Liu Shaoqi. An ever-increasing number of editorials, grasping for political power, still fuel public concern that "newspapers rule the nation" and "editorials run the country."

Journalists, however, do not bear sole responsibility for this development. Our Party leaders have asked the newspapers to maintain an administrative attitude and tone. But Party leaders were able to do so only because our news mechanism permitted it to happen.

Since the Cultural Revolution has been impugned, this practice has become indefensible. Yet for various reasons, the tendency still exists for newspapers to assume Party and government authority or a judicial tone, rather than playing their intended role.

Why, after the General Principles of Civil Law took effect in 1987, were so many lawsuits brought and won against journalists and the mass media? When a reformed society is operating under the principle that "everyone is equal before the law," the rights of news organizations *do not supersede* those of citizens, organizations, or other entities. The supervision of the social structure through public opinion to which the media are called must be carried out in such a way that it does not infringe upon the legal rights of others. Even Party newspapers, which have enjoyed enormous power, must now be meticulous with each article or risk facing lawsuits.

Open-minded journalists should celebrate such social development! They should not mourn the "good old days" or a past in which they wrote fierce editorials for Party papers without a thought to legal ramifications! Those days are gone. We cannot confuse the media's substantial intellectual influence with power to command society. More important, we should not think of the media as having any power superior to that of citizens and the proletariat.

A LACK OF CONSCIOUS RESPECT FOR THE INDIVIDUAL

Another important reason for press infringement is that China's media sometimes lack respect for the protection of human rights and human dignity. In a China immersed in several thousands of years of rigidly stratified feudalism, there is widespread insufficient awareness of human rights. Too often there is evidence of "bowing before the elite and strutting before the lowly." Modern mass media that advocate democracy and science should not succumb to the temptation to please the powerful, but they do. In the posture of "implementing public opinion supervision," newspapers wait for approval from the Party and government. Thus, the top directs the bottom, one level over another.

In the past, public criticism of certain negative archetypes was considered necessary to the success of a campaign or to the promotion of some project. But when such criticisms are publicized, and one person's behavior is held out as counterproductive to the goals of a specific campaign, that individual can be disproportionately and profoundly affected. Typically, he becomes the target of unrelenting criticism, and his shame becomes more notorious than the cause the original criticism was intended to promote. Throughout the process, the victim is typically denied any opportunity to answer the charges. Even in those cases where reporting errors have been discovered, the media have refused to make prompt, public corrections on the grounds that the campaign might be compromised.

Journalists have seemed to justify disregard for the individual because greater issues are at stake. They have taken solace in the belief that the interests of the group outweigh the interest of any individual. Injustices committed under this rationale were rampant in the not-too-distant past. He Long[17] was among the negative archetypes blasted in the media during the Cultural Revolution. But when the government exonerated him and announced the rehabilitation of his reputation, the newspapers would not report it. His reputation was not publicly restored until the Cultural Revolution was safely past. By that time, He Long had died.

Responsibility for that particular injustice surely lies with the senior news examiners rather than with the journalists themselves. But journalists must share some responsibility for such injuries. For example, in August 1984, *The Guangming Daily* published a series of articles criticizing Yao Qiana, the head of The Nanjing Natural Science Institute and a scholar of national and international reputation. Yao was accused of plagiarism and of taking credit for other scientist's research. The series was intended to support the current government policy on intellectuals, but the facts of the case were misinterpreted. Even though the reporters and the newspaper knew full well—both before and after the story's publication—that substantially different sets of facts were coming from the Jiangsu Provincial Propaganda and Cultural Bureaus, they still insisted on reporting only the Propaganda Bureau's point of view. The esteemed scientist was given no opportunity to argue on his own behalf, and the incident ultimately led to Yao Qian's death.

That reporter's primary motive may have been to promote what he thought would be a compelling prototype to help implement the Party's policies and so counter unhealthy escalation. But even that rationale cannot be allowed to obfuscate the severe injury his series caused the targeted intellectual. Ruining an accomplished man through unsubstantiated rumors is not simply "the price that must be paid."

THE DEARTH OF FAIR AND OBJECTIVE REPORTING

Objective and fair reporting have never been part of news reporting in China. During China's several thousand years of feudalism and centralized power, writers—fearing what could be catastrophic ramifications—had to be very careful. They often used euphemisms and implications to reflect their own opinions. A few acerbic articles with strong wording found their way into print, but they were rare and usually appeared only during special periods.

China's modern newspaper were born as the Qing Dynasty deteriorated. People's long-restrained objections to the feudalistic regime poured out when they discovered a natural outlet in the newspapers. Since then, a revolutionary, combative writing style has dominated China's newspapers and magazines—from Liang Qichao's timely political comments whose "words often pulled forth emotions";[18] to the pointed phrase "turmoil, a good medicine to save China" that first appeared in the *Dajiang Newspaper* two months before the Wuchang Uprising;[19] to Lu Xun's essays, with images of "to flog the cur that had fallen into the water."[20] All were riveting articles that sharply denounced enemies and all that is ugly. They remain a joy to read.

After the establishment of the People's Republic of China, as major political campaigns surfaced, one after another, the sensational writing style was still in demand. Regretfully, those political campaigns often proved misguided and claimed too many victims. Anyone from the president of the country to ordinary workers could be impugned as "capitalist representatives," "royalists," "royalist dogs," "chameleons," and "small reptiles."[21] The Chinese who suffered through it now concur that the Cultural Revolution should be denounced, but have not yet reached agreement as to what extent modern journalists should retain that combative writing style in a new day of peaceful construction and economic development.

There are two reasons why the situation today is completely different from revolutionary times. First, the purpose of revolution is to acquire political power, so using sensational writing to encourage chaos in the social order was helpful to the revolution. But now we are building the country, and developing the economy and a democratic political system. Stability and order require a simple, objective news style. Second, there were no laws to protect common citizens in the past. When a newspaper wronged an individual, the victim had little recourse. Today, the victim can turn to the courts for justice.

GOVERNMENT SUPERVISION THROUGH PUBLIC OPINION

No discussion of media infringement upon reputation and privacy would be complete without an analysis of the role of the mass media in government supervision through public opinion. The government uses the informative function of the media to help the public understand governmental policy and public affairs. Public opinion supervision, conversely, uses the power of uncensored, responsible, published public opinion to keep government actions in conformity with the law and with the guiding principles of social life. A modern society depends on this balance for its very existence.

Reports that convey information about, and comment upon, government and public matters are very important to this process. They are also the very same articles that tend to engender defamation suits. So any discussion of defamation suits must address this question: How can the media's right to carry out *public opinion supervision* be protected?

Article 38 of China's Constitution stipulates: "The personal dignity of citizens of the People's Republic of China is inviolable. Insult, libel, false accusation or false incrimination directed against citizens by any means is prohibited."[22] Article 131[23] and 146[24] of the Criminal Law, and Article 101,[25] 102[26] and 120[27] of the General Principles of Civil Law are all detailed, constitutionally based regulations. They enable people to invoke specific legal regulations when relevant individual, corporate, or entity disputes occur.

Although China's Constitution provides that "citizens of People's Republic of China have the right to criticize and make suggestions regarding any state organ or functionary,"[28] there are no specific regulations that guarantee this principle's implementation. So when the courts consider cases involving defamation by the news media, they can refer only to Criminal Law and Civil Law. Because they have no *specific* legal precedent, the courts cannot sufficiently protect the media's right to public opinion supervision. Hence, the demand is accelerating—from press circles, legal circles, and society as a whole—for a press law as the only way to provide the detailed regulations the courts will need to adjudicate such cases.

To date, China's public opinion supervision is still in its initial stage of development. Thus far, most of China's public opinion supervision has dealt only with the lowest level of government employees and common citizens. Oversight of the upper echelons—such as government policy and the political activities of senior government officials—is far from adequate. Even though such reports are the most likely to stimulate infringement and slander charges, public supervision reporting at every level should be encouraged.

EMPOWERING AND PROTECTING PUBLIC OPINION SUPERVISION

The above analysis shows that China's current practice of public opinion supervision through the media is inadequate. If a workable, beneficial public opinion supervision model is to be implemented, the following efforts should be made.

Society Should Venerate and Protect Public Opinion Supervision

There is inherent difficulty in conducting public opinion supervision. News activity stresses timeliness, which makes errors unavoidable. Moreover, it is relatively difficult for reporters to gather facts and quotations, since news interviews (in contrast to the survey information prepared by judicial and administrative organs) depend upon a voluntary act by the interviewee. It is, therefore, impractical to demand error-free public opinion supervision.

Members of a developed society, especially government officials in the public trust at every level, should develop a deep respect for the significant influence that public opinion supervision has upon the enlightened operation of politics, society, and the country's development. Benevolence should be the measure when the injury caused by the media is a minor one. When the damage is more serious, the complaint should first be made directly to the media and, where appropriate, a published correction requested before turning to the courts. Along this line, the Danish press law stipulates: "If a magazine article causes an individual significant financial or reputation injury, the publication's editors are obligated to publish the requested correction without changes and without charge."[29] It follows that if the injury is insignificant, then the publication need not publish a correction or go to court to answer a lawsuit.

In Adjudication of News Disputes, Careful Consideration Should Be Given to the Balance Between Citizens' Right to Their Reputation and the Media's Right to Public Opinion Supervision

Greenwood and Welsh of Great Britain have articulated the Western perspective on this critical balance: "Slander law should keep the balance between protecting individual reputation and protecting speech free-dom."[30] To protect public opinion supervision, judicial organs should operate within the following parameters:

Refuse to hear lawsuits involving insignificant injury

When a complainant brings a lawsuit, the court should pay attention not only to whether or not the facts are clear, or if there is sufficient evidence to support a charge of defamation, but also to the degree of damage. If the injury is insignificant, the court should explain to the litigant the meaning and purpose of public opinion supervision and per-suade him to withdraw the lawsuit or change his pleading. Such expla-nation and persuasion cannot be considered infringement upon the litigant's right of action.

Distinguish charges against moral behavior from those against job performances

If the media criticize an individual's moral behavior (e.g., labeling him a thief, hooligan, swindler), thereby injuring his reputation, the injury is usually severe and should be dealt with in the courts. By comparison, if the case is such that the media inaccurately report that someone made a mistake at a job site or did poor work, that injury is relatively insig-nificant. In the latter case, the news outlet should be required only to apologize and publish a correction. The courts should take care that they do not rashly accept "poor performance" cases—as in cases where the news media criticize the poor performance of some branch of govern-ment. News media have the right to comment, and citizens have the right to praise or to criticize something through the media, even if those com-ments occasionally conflict with the facts.

Distinguish secondhand commentary from the original report

Reporting is about discovering the facts of a story. When the principle facts in a report have been proven to be false and harmful to a litigant's reputation, the matter should be treated seriously. However, when a reader uses the media to make a secondhand comment on the initial report—as is their constitutional right—that writer should be distin-guished from the original news reporter, even though such comments might further damage the litigant's reputation. The plaintiff's right to choose the defendant is not sufficient pretext for excusing the author of the original report, as has happened in the past.[31]

Endeavor to give relatively light penalties and punishments

Those proven to have slandered with malice should receive severe punishment. However, when reputation infringement is caused by a story whose facts are accurate but incomplete, or when the story's errors have been made by individuals other than the writer during the editing or interviewing process, the defendant should not be subject to harsh punishment. Indeed, in some cases, greater leniency may be more appropriate.

This flexibility is especially necessary today, when China's public opinion supervision is still in its difficult initial stages. Courts are awarding damages that are disproportionate to the offense. In one case, the author of a comprehensive feature article on the development of sports in China was fined two thousand yuan simply because the article made a minor error in a person's name. The error caused no obvious injury to the person mentioned.

Distinguish damage awards according to punitive and compensatory damages

This distinction is fairly obvious. Some malicious slander is severe, even though it does not result in economic damage or obvious mental injury. In such cases, the defendant should pay a relatively high punitive award in addition to any reasonable damages for mental injury.

Infringement to reputation is often from unexpected error or carelessness. Still, the person wronged suffers considerable injury to his reputation. In this situation, the defendant should pay a high compensatory award and either modest or no punitive damages. Such a distinction can help the media learn from experience, even as it helps society understand what should be protected, what should be opposed, and what should be forgiven. It will also promote informed understanding of public opinion supervision.[32]

We Yongzheng[33]—writing for the State Press and Publication Administration's 1993 treatise on "Public Opinion Supervision and News Disputes"—articulates two important conditions for legal proceedings against news organizations and their members:

a. Establish the principle that in order to initiate legal proceedings against someone for alleged news infringement, the plaintiff must provide evidence that:

    1. the news report has been published;

    2. the plaintiff is the person involved in the news report;

    3. the content of the news report runs counter to fact or has infringement characteristics, such as insulting the targeted person or invading privacy;

    4. the defendant has conducted the action intentionally, if the plaintiff is a government employee; and

    5. the action has caused injury to the plaintiff.

Only when all these have been established should the court put the case on file for investigation and prosecution.

b. A government employee cannot demand that a news reporter bear civil responsibility for infringement unless he has been the subject of purposeful injury, that is to say slander or insult.... In incidents of unintentional injury to a government employee (absent slander or insult), the media can compensate by publishing a correction or response. If the media involved refuse to do so, then the affected government employee can resort to the court for a legal judgment requiring the media to publish correction and response. If it cannot be proved that errors by the news reporter were deliberate, then the plaintiff cannot demand an apology or compensation from the media or the news reporter.[34]

NOTES

1. *General Principles of the Civil Law of the People's Republic of China*, adopted at the Fourth Session of the Sixth National People's Congress, promulgated by Order No. 37 of the president of the People's Republic of China on April 12, 1986, and effective as of January 1, 1987. English translation, *China Law*, http://www.qis.net/chinalaw/lawtran1.htm.

2. *A Collection of Theses at the Seminar on News Disputes and Legal Responsibilities*, p. 177. Edited and published by the Institute of Journalism, Shanghai Academy of Social Sciences, 1992.

3. Ibid.

4. *Public Opinion Supervision and News Disputes—A Collection of Theses at the Second National News Disputes and Legal Responsibilities Seminar*, pp. 11–12. Edited by the Policy and Regulations Department of the State Press and Publication Administration, 1993.

5. Ibid.

6. People's Judicature, No. 2, 1989.

7. The Du Rong, "20-year 'Mad Woman Riddle,' " lawsuit was filed against Shen Yafu and Mo Chunlin, reporters for *Minzhu Yu Fazhi (Democracy and the Rule of Law)*, a legal magazine based in Shanghai. The "Spirits of the Cultural Revolution are Strolling Here—an 'Earthquake' in the Shanghai Gramophone Record Company" suit by Li Baoshan and Zhouwei was brought against Shi Xinyuan. In the former case, the offending article accused Du (who was then living in Wuhan) of coercing his wife to feign mental illness as a pretext for allowing him to move to Shanghai, where she lived. The court dismissed the reporters' argument that they had no criminal intent and that their speech was protected by Article 35 of the Constitution. Both reporters were ordered to pay damages and deprived of political rights. Fu & Cullen, p. 189, citing Wei Yongzheng, Beigao Xishangde Jizhe (reporters on the defense), Shanghai People's Publisher 1994, pp. 3–5; and Hillary K. Josephs, "Defamation, Invasion of Privacy, and the Press in the People's Republic of China," 1993 *U.C.L.A. Pacific Basin Law Journal*, p. 191.

8. If the majority of the people surrounding the litigant believe the article

targets the specific person, then the author cannot avoid responsibility on the grounds of identification.

9. The Party's reasoning was that positive reports encourage and inspire the people; therefore, critical news should be reduced to avoid grievances and social upheaval.

10. "The Third Tide of News Lawsuits," *China Youth Newspaper*, August 5, 1993.

11. This district has the largest number of newspaper and magazine offices in China.

12. *China Encyclopedia* (law volume), p. 473.

13. *A Collection of Teaching Materials of the Senior Party School Directly Attached to the Center of the Soviet Union Communist Party*, p. 1, People's Publishing House, 1954.

14. *Selected Documents and Materials of Xinhua News Agency*, No. 2, p. 4, 1980, edited by the News Research Department of the Xinhua News Agency.

15. The thought-reform campaigns against intellectuals in the early 1950s.

16. See note 14.

17. He Long (1896–1969) was a member of the political bureau and vice premier.

18. Liang Qichao (1873–1929) was one of the great Confucian reformers of the late Qing and early revolutionary periods. A follower of Qing reformer Kang Yuwei, Liang is generally considered to represent the kind of radical reformism that paved the way to the Revolution of 1911. See, for example, De Bary et al., *Sources of Chinese Tradition* 2, p. 87, 1960.

19. The Wuchang Uprising of October 10, 1911, was triggered by a Qing crackdown against revolutionary activity in that city and led to the creation of a military government (under Li Yuanhung, a general of the Qing New Army), which gradually came under revolutionary influence. The new government declared the end of the Qing Dynasty and the establishment of the Republic of China.

20. Lu Xun (1881–1936) was one of the leading intellectuals in the iconoclastic New Culture Movement from roughly 1915 to 1927.

21. These derogatory terms used during the Cultural Revolution are listed by degrees of intensity from the strongest to the mildest.

22. Constitution of the People's Republic of China, Art. 38 (1982).

23. The author is referring to a provision of the Criminal Law that became effective January 1, 1980. "The rights of the person, democratic rights and other rights of citizens shall be protected from unlawful infringement by any person or organization. If the circumstances of unlawful infringement are serious, those directly responsible shall be given criminal sanctions." This version of the Criminal Law was superseded in 1997. The essence of this provision is now found in Article 2 of the Criminal Law of the People's Republic of China (March 14, 1997).

24. From the 1980 Criminal Law: "Any state functionary who abuses his power, using his public office for private gain, in order to retaliate against or frame complainants, petitioners or critics or incriminate them on false charges shall be sentenced to a fixed-term imprisonment . . ." Article 243 of the 1997 Criminal Law contains similar provisions.

25. Citizens and corporations shall enjoy the right of reputation. Reputation

shall be protected by law, and the use of insults, libel, or other means that damage the reputation of citizens or corporations shall be prohibited.

26. Citizens and corporations shall enjoy the right of tribute. It shall be prohibited to unlawfully divest citizens and legal persons of their honorary titles.

27. If a citizen's right of personal name, likeness, reputation, or honor is infringed upon, he shall have the right to demand that the infringement be stopped, his reputation be rehabilitated, the ill effects be eliminated and an apology be made; he may also demand compensation for losses. The above paragraph shall also apply to infringements upon a legal person's right of name, reputation, or honor.

28. Constitution, Art. 41.

29. "Selections of Press and Publication Laws of Different Countries," p. 132, People's Daily Publishing House.

30. Ibid., pp. 220–21.

31. In 1995, store guards suspected two women of shoplifting at China's World Trade Center and searched them. *The Beijing Youth News* reported the incident. In response to the article, a playwright wrote an editorial that criticized the World Trade Center. The World Trade Center sued the playwright, but not the newspaper.

32. "Public Opinion Supervision and News Disputes," pp. 4–48. Compiled by the Policy and Regulations Department of the State Press and Publication Administration in 1993.

33. The second researcher in China to write on press law.

34. "Public Opinion Supervision and News Disputes," pp. 37, 38–39. Compiled by the Policy and Regulations Department of the State Press and Publication Administration in 1993.

CHAPTER 11

The Viability of Limited Public Ownership and Interregional Development

The formal media system under which China has been operating for some time places newspapers and television stations under the sole jurisdiction of government offices. This system is counterproductive, for both China and her citizens. Not only is progress stifled by undue political influence and limited freedom, but a government-bound system is inefficient and a poor use of resources.

Now that the reform of China's economic system is nearly complete, we have occasion to consider how our media system might be transformed into a more self-sufficient, cost-effective, and efficient information industry.

At a Hong Kong Baptist University seminar in June 1998, titled "Asian News Media and Social Change," I presented my thesis "China's News Media Need New Approaches and New Policies." What follows is the first chapter of that paper, in which I make five recommendations: (*a*) the amount of governmental administration must be reduced; (*b*) market self-adjustment must be allowed to have its effect; (*c*) newspaper groups must be allowed to participate in China's emerging public shareholding system; (*d*) broader media development must be encouraged throughout the country; and (*e*) the restrictions binding China's media to governmental offices must be abolished. Until 1999, China's news media were forbidden from participating in the new public ownership system and from expanding distribution across provincial lines. In that year, however, the public ownership system was applied to the official newspaper of the Harbin Municipal Party Committee. Representatives from more than 100 newspapers traveled there to observe the model. Soon after, my article was permitted publication in *Circle of Journalism* 11, 1999.

China's news media now exist on a grand scale. By 1996, China boasted 2,163 newspapers, almost twelve times the number in 1978.[1] Among them are such titans as *The Liberation Daily*, a 20-page,[2] province-level, Party committee–run, daily newspaper; *The Guangzhou Daily*, a 40-page, city-level, Party committee–run newspaper; and the 32-page, daily *Xinmin Evening News*.

By 1997, China had 8,135 magazines and 1,416 radio stations. Compared with the corresponding numbers from 1976, these represent an 800 percent and 1,500 percent increase, respectively. By 1994, China already had 3,125 officially sanctioned TV stations, not including the tens of thousands of cable stations that operate without official permission. This dramatic figure is double that of the United States, 25 times that of Japan, and 260 times the figure in the United Kingdom. It surpasses the combined number (2,606) in the United States, Russia, Japan, Great Britain, France, Germany, India, Canada, Australia, Brazil, and Pakistan.[3]

However—to put this in perspective—most of China's 3,125 registered TV stations are very small in scale, capable of producing only a limited number of TV programs. Even when these stations have the most advanced equipment—as a few do—their station personnel lack even the most basic of training. Their best efforts, their "exhibition programs," are so dreadful that they have no entertainment value whatsoever.[4]

CHINA'S OFFICIAL MEDIA SYSTEM HAS FOLLOWED A POLICY OF PERPETUAL EXPANSION

China is a large country with limited resources. What natural resources it has are often wasted. Waste of news media resources is even more pronounced. Although the total number of newspapers has increased 1,100 percent in twenty years, total circulation has only doubled. The average circulation of any given newspaper in 1996 was only about 18.5 percent of the 1978 figure.

The subsequent drain on public funds is considerable. At the beginning of 1997, China had more than 3,000 government-approved TV stations, including cable. The approximate cost for construction of one county-level TV station is 10 million yuan (U.S.$1.2 million). Once a station is up and running, yearly operating expenses can easily exceed 1 million yuan (U.S.$120,000). This is an onerous burden on the still-deficit budgets of local governments.[5]

Current guidelines let any governmental organization run an authorized media outlet; China's Radio and Television Policy clearly states that each of the four levels of government (central, provincial, city, and county) have the privilege of running their own radio or TV stations. This means that any recognized organization may run a newspaper or establish a TV or radio station without accounting for the social demand for its information, the saturation limits of the information industry, or the economic efficiency of investment and yields. Allocation of funds is justified under the premise of "publicizing that organization's 'good deeds.' " This trend perpetuates itself ad infinitum.

Recent efforts by the Information Administrative Department to remedy this situation have failed. In the past ten years, the State has rectified[6] its newspaper publication policies three times. The first rectification took place in 1978, when 270 of the 1,761 openly published newspapers were closed down.[7] The second was carried out in October 1989, when the government disbanded 190 of the 1,682 official newspapers.[8] The third rectification lasted for three years, from 1996 to 1998. In that time, 300 officially published papers were shut down.[9]

Meanwhile, most "inside" or "restricted" papers—those published only for Party or government officials or cadres—were either closed down or recategorized as reference materials. By 1997, more than 4,000 of them had been cut from the initial 60,000.[10]

In 1997, the number of radio stations was also reduced. In Jiangsu Province alone, 97 of the 212 radio stations were closed down.[11] Hunan Province shut down 210 of their 402 stations.[12]

Despite these efforts, every rectification or streamlining was followed by a new surge in development.

In recent years, the State Press and Publication Administration has attempted to regulate the number of new newspapers. Under these new guidelines, each province is limited to two or three additional newspapers in a year, with the stipulation that a corresponding number are closed down. However, China's rapid economic development and the fast growth of advertising exacerbate the collective penchant for publicity, and provincial press administrations find it hard to refuse or prevent applications.

Once a new paper is approved and set up, any number of official organizations provide free financial support—even if the paper is run inefficiently—and the sponsoring organizations either require their subordinate units to subscribe or force them to buy advertising space. It is very rare for a newspaper to fold because of financial problems. Clearly, an official media system that runs newspapers with public funds and then uses public money to pay for reader subscriptions perpetuates a situation in which publications "exist forever and never die."

By contrast, the newspapers sold at stands on city streets are run quite differently. Because readers must spend their own money for these papers, survival depends upon caliber of content. However, this dynamic is not yet part of the discussion. The governmental organizations that run the larger papers publish these papers—more than ninety of them—as "sidelines" to build unit morale. Consequently, the profit they make and the process by which they do it is dismissed.[13]

This system can only beget itself. The larger it grows, the more sluggish China's media will become. The current policy of "compulsory control over the total number of newspapers" provides no room for the newspapers that should be set up. A vicious circle is formed, as "those which ought to die would not die, while those which ought to be born could not be born."

The pattern is a familiar one. Under the planned economic system, local governments were keen both to start new projects and to expand old ones. The result was a glut of inefficient overnight start-ups. In an effort to address the situation, the government implemented a series of readjustment and rectification programs that closed down the start-ups and laid off their personnel. Administrative decree was the sole impetus for initiation or closure. All of these programs came to no avail.

Then, in the process of building a market economy, it dawned on us that, if we are to break this vicious cycle, we must use economic methods to handle the economy. All our efforts to encourage enterprise must go to applying the "market self-adjustment" approach, following the rule of "survival of the fittest."

THE NEWS BUSINESS WOULD BENEFIT FROM PARTICIPATING IN THE NEW PUBLIC OWNERSHIP MODEL AND FROM EXPANDING SERVICE ACROSS REGIONS AND PROFESSIONS

The market economy's development strategy might also suit the needs of our news media. Until now, we have been managing the process of media reform by administrative decree. Instead, we should take a lesson from what has been effective in the development of our socialist market economy and turn to appropriate economic and market strategies.

In June 1993, the Central Committee of the Chinese Communist Party and the State Council publicized their "Decision on Escalating Development of the Tertiary Industries."[14] The committee's official classification of newspaper management as one of the tertiary *industries* marked a turning point in the reform of our news media.[15] As a central component of the information industry, the news media rightly belongs under this classification and should be so classified, both in our research and in all the decisions that bear upon future construction and development. Unless our news media achieve parity with the information industries in developed countries, China will not be able to participate in the fast-paced world information environment; our leaders will be unable to make timely and efficient decisions; nor will we have the capacity to produce first-class entrepreneurs or world-class enterprises.

The way to build our news media into a modern information industry is to apply exactly the same principles that developed the market economy. The argument that "news media should be kept clear of the new shareholding system" does not hold water.

It is widely accepted that China's news media have become increasingly industrial over the last twenty years. In recent industrial reform, State enterprises—still the mainstay of the economy—coexist with multiple-owner enterprises. In these new multiple-owner industries, the State retains the majority of the shares, but the remainder are exchanged on the formal stock market.[16]

It would be easy to test this principle in the news media. A few of the more established publications in key cities could serve as experiments. They could be run in such a way that the State would act as majority stockholder, while citizens or corporations managed actual publication. The Constitutional tenet that "citizens have the freedom of speech and publication" would be satisfied, and the news media could perform their social role in a comparatively independent way. It would also serve to curb indiscriminate expansion of government- and officially-protected news media.[17]

The people who are decrying shareholding in the media industry are the same ones who argued against public ownership when it was first introduced in the market economy. Yet in spite of those objections, the fifteenth National Congress of the Chinese Communist Party gave its full endorsement to the shareholding system. General Secretary Jiang Zemin pointed out in his report: "The stock-holding system provides a structure by which modern enterprises can obtain capital. [It] is conducive to the separation of ownership and management rights and to improving enterprise efficiency and capital operation—beneficial concepts which can be utilized by capitalism as well as socialism."[18]

TWO PREVAILING CONDITIONS COMPEL ADOPTION OF THE SHAREHOLDING SYSTEM

The rationale for this goes beyond replication of the economic model. Two prevailing conditions[19] compel the news media to adopt a shareholding system: (1) the emergence of newspaper groups with abundant financial resources, and (2) a geographical imbalance in the news media's development.

A number of media units are eager to experiment with shareholding. At least one newspaper has quietly done it.

The Zhejiang Province *Jinhua Daily* began converting to a shareholding system early in 1994, with assets divided among three sectors: state, work group, and individual. Each operation functions separately. For example, the editorial department's only task is to make the newspaper better, and development decisions are made according to the indications of modern enterprise. Here, as in other applications, the concept of gradual introduction of the shareholding system into all state-owned enterprises is now accepted as common sense.

From its first day, the success of *The Harbin Daily Press* Group Joint Stock Company has attracted considerable traffic. The 1999 Conference on Deepening Newspaper Reforms was held in Harbin from September 9 through September 12. Participants from 104 newspapers listened to *The Harbin Daily's* reform experience, which served to substantiate a number of important principles. Among them:

- the most effective guidance of public opinion will be implemented in partnership with the market;
- newspapers were acknowledged to have a specific market;
- the acknowledgement that Party newspapers must be marketed confirmed newspapers as commodities;
- newspaper offices were shown to be enterprises;
- newspaper management was characterized as an industry.

The conference proposed that "Newspapers should be run by statesmen, managed by entrepreneurs, and should serve society under the market system." Although this recommendation for media reform still "treats the symptoms but not the disease," it does pave the way for a comprehensive set of standards based upon partnership among the media, the market economy, and international practice.

The Harbin Daily's economic structure centers around a shareholding company based upon a modern enterprise system. As soon as it received its initial corporate classification, this press group was able to operate like an enterprise, with capital management, multi-channel investment, and operation under a corporate identity. *The Harbin Daily's* experience will not work for every media entity, but its outcomes are of unilateral significance.

Two emerging factors offer the conditions necessary to establish and run publicly owned news media: (1) the advent of thriving newspaper groups and (2) the lopsided rates of development among news entities.

The Emergence of Media Groups

The 1990s trend toward media groups has paved the way for public ownership. The first such group, *The Guangzhou Daily* Newspaper Group,

Table 11.1
Advertising Impact on the daily *Xinmin Evening News* **1996/1998**

Year	Per Issue Publication Cost	Per Issue Selling Price	Per Issue Pages & Special Features
1996	0.9 yuan ($.07 US)	0.5 yuan ($.04 US)	24 pages
1998	1.6 yuan ($.13 US)	0.5 yuan ($.04 US)	32 pages + color printing

Table 11.2
Advertising Impact on the *Liberation Daily* **1996/1998**

Year	Per Issue Publication Cost	Per Issue Selling Price	Per Issue Pages & Special Features
1996	1.1 yuan ($.09 US)	0.6 yuan ($.05 US)	12 pages
1998	1.9 yuan ($.15 US)	0.6 yuan ($.05 US)	20 pages

was officially sanctioned in January 1996. After some internal modifications, it evolved from a single news media unit into several units with related enterprises. Now, the group boasts ten newspapers, one magazine, a news service center, a newspaper distribution company, a chain store, and a real estate company. In 1995, their total business income was 800 million yuan (U.S. $100 million), of which half[20] came from its flagship's[21] advertising. Since then, five other newspaper groups have been formed and sanctioned.

There are also numerous de facto newspaper groups (such as *Liberation Daily, Sichuan Daily, Zhejiang Daily*), all of which are thriving economically. Others (such as *The Shenzhen Special Zone Daily* and *Beijing Youth Daily*) are not considered to be actual newspaper groups, although each profitably manages several newspapers, institutions, and enterprises.

Recently, moneymaking newspapers have discovered that it is possible to distribute their papers below cost. For instance, in 1996, single issues of both *The Xinmin Evening News* and *The Liberation Daily* sold at half the cost of publishing. By 1998, the low costs held constant, even though *The Xinmin Evening News* added a third again as many pages and color (see Table 11.1). In the same time period, *The Liberation Daily* nearly doubled in size and yet still sold for the below-cost, single-issue price of two years before (see Table 11.2).

These newspapers have entered a "virtuous" circle. Increased readership brings in more advertising. Then, as the paper becomes more affordable to the person on the street, readership again increases. Readers have been swarming to papers such as *The Xinmin Evening News, Guangzhou Daily*, and *The Yangcheng Evening News*. These papers are finding themselves in a much more lucrative position as—in some cases—advertisers are having to wait in line.

And unlike most Chinese newspapers, these newspapers are not com-

pelled to give advertising kickbacks. Nor must they contend with reporters who neglect their work to chase advertising commissions.

Regional Imbalance

A second condition compels this reform. In the past ten years, the
regional imbalance of news media development between the southeast
coastal regions and the rest of the country has become more and more
pronounced. Dramatic illustration is offered in the disparity among advertising incomes.

In 1993, of the eight newspapers that brought in more than 100 million
yuan (U.S. $12 million) in advertising revenue, three were from Guang-
dong Province,[22] two from Shanghai,[23] and one from Hainan Province.[24]
Yet among China's vast northern regions, only *The Beijing Evening News*
in the capital edged itself into the top eight.

In 1994, five newspapers surpassed 200 million yuan (U.S. $24 million)
in advertising income, but three of them were from Gaungdong[25] and
two were from Shanghai.[26] No northern or western papers reached the
mark.

The trend continued. By 1997, all top-five money earners were from
the coastal area.

The advantages of modern publishing equipment are also to be found
along the affluent coast. One evening newspaper in eastern China purchased seven sets of complete-course, rotating, computerized offset
presses from Germany at the cost of $20 million (U.S.), an astronomical
figure to newspapers in central and western China.

There is also great disparity in staff salaries. Many reporters and assistant editors in southeastern coastal papers earn around 5,000 to 7,000
yuan (U.S. $600 to $850) per month, whereas the staff at radio stations
in western China earn one-tenth as much—less than 500 yuan (U.S. $60)
per month. Unchecked, this situation will inevitably lead to brain drain
from the west.

This imbalance causes a dilemma. Recent research testifies, "Some media entities have no way to raise the money they need. Others with
surplus capital are not permitted to invest in undercapitalized media
through stock transactions, [and so] their only option is to invest in industries with which they are unfamiliar, resulting in serious losses."[27]

Publication of Interregional Newspapers

How can the assets, technology, and know-how enjoyed by China's
developed coastal areas be introduced inland to promote development
of their news media? The obvious solution is twofold: implement a share-

holding system and publish interregional newspapers through joint efforts.

The media must be allowed to expand and develop in other administrative regions. That is, the media in one region should be allowed to run media in other regions and to report news there. In the short time since *Heilongjiang Old-Age Newspaper* changed its name to *The Old-Age Newspaper*, it has become China's largest newspaper for the aged, with the largest circulation.

China covers a vast territory; each region has its own economic characteristics and trends. If a newspaper were to specialize in timely, regional, economic information, it would dramatically and positively impact both the developing information industry and China's market economy as a whole. The advantage of such a paper—simultaneously released in editions for the economic regions of south China, east China, central China, north China, northwest China, and southwest China—is self-evident.

Certainly, the State cannot be expected to shoulder the management and sponsorship of such publications, but China's thriving newspaper groups have both the motivation and the capacity. The State need only grant permission for interregional expansion and development.

If interregional media expansion is realized, the results will likely be impressive. It is entirely possible that economic papers every bit as influential as *The Japanese Economic News* or *The Financial Times of London* could some day appear on China's newsstands. Many in China believe that publications of that caliber could emerge from China's own newspaper groups.

Similar Development Is Appropriate for Radio and Television

The system of television in China operates at four levels of authority: central, provincial, city, and country. These delineations once played an important historical role, but now—because the labyrinth of restrictions from any number of government agencies serves mainly to constrain the media—it is almost impossible for broadcast media to develop rapidly. This situation calls for immediate reform.

The competitive condition inherent in the international broadcasting industry demands that we quicken the pace. Developed countries are already implementing Asia marketing strategies, and China is the focal point of those efforts.

China wants to participate in the World Trade Organization (WTO), which, among other things, would require the gradual loosening of market control on audiovisual products. Because of the rapid development of our economy, China owns more televisions than any other country in the world. As soon as WTO membership is granted, China must abide by generally accepted principles and open her [broad-based] telecommunication market. If we use old ways to deal with these new circumstances amid fierce international competition, we will lose.

In the long term, the television industry should adopt a shareholding system, with the state-owned Central China Television at its core. At the same time, a number of large electronic communications groups should be established in China.

I submit that television in China should no longer serve exclusively as a propaganda tool for specific government departments, but should be managed as an industry. Some people are of the opinion that television will continue to best serve society as the propaganda tool for the Party and as the government's tool to counteract boycotting. If that is the standard, then television will never be able to develop as an industry. Such people do not realize that—as the socialist market system develops—the mass media will become more and more dynamic; they will no longer blindly obey government rules that tell them what to do and what not to do, but obey and serve mainstream ideology within the limits of the Constitution and law.

RECOMMENDATIONS

Policies currently in effect should be adjusted to promote development of the mass communication industry. First, permission should be given for major communications groups to establish shareholding entities in several economically progressive areas across the country. These groups can be made up entirely of television stations, or certain groups could align television with telecommunication, computer, or other industries. The pervasive influence of this medium should move us to speedy and cooperative action.

The market-traded Dianguang Industry—formerly The Radio and Television Development Center under the Human Province Department of Broadcasting and Television—has been listed in Shenzhen stock since March 1999. The operation has realized profit in excess of 400 million yuan (U.S. $50 million).

China's only traded broadcasting corporation to date, the Dianguang Industry, is thriving—impressive evidence of the boundless opportunity in this field. As of this writing, however, there is still no evidence of plans for a traded multi-media group that unites television, telecommunications, and computer technology. But it will come into being one day.

There is abiding truth to the saying "That which is essential will eventually find its way into practice."

NOTES

1. 11.84

2. Most major Chinese newspapers are four to eight pages in length.

3. Wang Jianhong, "How Many TV Stations China Should Build Exactly," in *Chinese Journalists* 5, 1996.

4. Xie Jinwen, "On China's News Media Market and Its Development," doctoral thesis, May 1998.

5. *South Weekend*, May 16, 1997. Fudan University, Shanghai.

6. Revamped

7. 15.4 percent.

8. 11.7 percent.

9. 15 percent.

10. Speech by Liang Heng, vice director of the State Press and Publication Administration, published in *Press and Publication Paper*, January 22, 1998.

11. 45.8 percent. *News World* 9 p. 41, 1997.

12. 52.2 percent. *Wenhui Daily*, December 12, 1997.

13. Sun Xupei, "The Commercial Development of China's News Media," in *Journalism Tribune* 2, 1997.

14. "Tertiary industries" refers to China's "Third-level" service industries. Agriculture is first; manufacturing (materials production) is second; and services are third—they include commerce, food services, tourism, finance, insurance, communications, education, and others.

15. Classifying the news media as an "industry" gives it high priority for reform and modernization.

16. Sun holds that a gradual shift to a market economy is appropriate to China's current conditions. Some news outlets would remain State-controlled; others would have part of their shares sold on the stock market. This "share-holding system" sets in motion the long-range possibility of more and more of each entity's shares being sold to the private sector, as that revenue stream proves to support the news outlet in question. In that way, the cycle of inefficiency would be broken. The strategy supports Sun's stand for gradual media reform.

17. "News Media Law Still Not in Sight after 18 Years' Hard Work" in *Chinese Reform Paper*, April 3, 1998.

18. *Modern Advertisement* 2, p. 12, 1997.

19. By "conditions," Sun means the factors must be in place.

20. 400 million yuan (U.S. $50 million).

21. *The Guangzhou Daily.*

22. *Guangzhou Daily, South Daily*, and *Yangcheng Daily.*

23. *Liberation Daily* and *Xinmin Evening News.*

24. *Hainan Daily.*

25. *Guangzhou Daily, South Daily*, and *Yangcheng Daily.*

26. *Liberation Daily* and *Xinmin Evening News.*

27. Xie Jinwen, "On China's News Media Market and Its Development," doctoral thesis, May 1998. Fudan University, Shanghai.

Suggested Readings

Chang, Won Ho, *Mass Media in China: The History and the Future* (Iowa State University Press, 1989)

Chen, Albert H. Y., *An Introduction to the Legal System of the People's Republic of China* (Butterworths Asia, 1992)

Des Forges, Roger V., Luo Ning, Wu Yen-bo, eds., *Chinese Democracy and the Crisis of 1989: Chinese and American Reflections* (State University of New York Press, 1993)

Fu, H. L., and Richard Cullen, *Media Law in the PRC* (Asia Law & Practice Publishing Ltd., 1996)

Grieder, Jerome B., *Intellectuals and the State in Modern China: A Narrative History* (The Free Press, 1981)

Huevel, Jon Vanden, and Everette E. Dennis, *The Unfolding Lotus: East Asia's Changing Media* (The Freedom Forum Media Studies Center, 1993)

Lee, Chin-Chuan, ed., *Voices of China: The Interplay of Politics and Journalism* (The Guilford Press, 1990)

Ogden Suzanne, Kathleen Hartford, Lawrence Sullivan and David Zweig, eds., *China's Search for Democracy: The Student and Mass Movement of 1989* (M. E. Sharpe, Inc., 1992)

Index

Entries followed by "n." refer to a note in the text; entries followed by "t" refer to a table.

About the Author and Editor

SUN XUPEI is Senior Research Fellow and Professor of Journalism at the graduate school of the Chinese Academy of Social Sciences' Institute of Journalism and Communication. He was editor of the Huaibei Bureau of Mining's *Miners News* and is also author of *New Treatise on Journalism* (1994). Sun served as Director of the Media Law Research Office and Director of the Institute of Journalism and Communication at the Chinese Academy of Social Sciences.

ELIZABETH C. MICHEL is a Visiting Professor of Communication at Kennesaw State University and President of Kairos Communicating Strategies, Incorporated. Michel is author of the *Kairos Communicating Process* (1998) and the *Kairos Communicating Strategies Interactive CD-ROM* (2000). She served as Communication Department Chair at Mars Hill College and as Visiting Scholar to the Institute of Journalism and Communication at the Chinese Academy of Social Sciences.